How to Help
Your Teenager
Find the
Right Career

How to Help Your Teenager Find the Right Career

CHARLES J. SHIELDS

College Entrance Examination Board, New York

Acknowledgments

Many thanks to my colleagues at Homewood-Flossmoor High School, Flossmoor, Illinois. Special thanks to Eleanor Steiner, librarian and career specialist; to Sandy Sullivan, gentle, devoted friend and caregiver; to my father for his encouragement and advice; to Cal Hainzinger, school psychologist; and to Carolyn Trager, my editor at the College Board, for making major contributions to the scope and purpose of this book.

Copies of this book are available from your local bookseller or may be ordered from College Board Publications, Box 886, New York, New York 10101–0886. The price is $12.95.

Editorial inquiries concerning this book should be directed to Editorial Office, The College Board, 45 Columbus Avenue, New York, New York 10023–6992.

Library of Congress Catalog Number: 88–070583
ISBN: 0–87447–305–5

Printed in the United States of America

9 8 7 6 5 4 3 2 1

Contents

Introduction: How To Use This Book

How important is it for young people to explore careers? Here's a story I like to tell parents.

One day a student came by my office in the guidance department and said she would like to participate in Take-A-Kid-To-Work, a job-shadowing program I coordinate in which students spend one day following a worker of their choice.

"I really think I want to be a dietician," she said.

As it turned out, I had a dietician on my list of adult volunteers, so I was able to send the girl out to a site the next day. A few days later, she dropped in again.

"Well, how was it?" I asked. "Did you have fun?"

"Don't ever send me there again," she said.

I hardly knew what to say. "Did something bad happen?"

She tapped her foot impatiently. "Do you know what they had me do most of the day?" she said. *"They had me work in the kitchen! Do you believe it? And I asked for a dietician."*

My impulse was to say, Well, what did you expect? That's where a dietician spends a lot of her time! Instead I suggested, "Now at least you know what you *don't* want to do, and that's pretty important, too."

As the career counselor in a high school of 2,400 students, I've learned that whether students seem to have definite career goals or are still uncertain about their future work, exploring careers should be part of their plans. Otherwise, choices tend to be based on impressions instead of facts, as in the case of the girl who misunderstood what a dietician does.

xi

In addition, exploring careers makes clear the importance of meeting certain job requirements, or presents entirely new opportunities. For instance, I often have young men and women tell me they want to fly planes in the Air Force or the Navy. Many of them don't realize that higher mathematics plays a big role in a pilot's education. Some of these students don't even like math, so after their initial disappointment passes, I try to redirect their interest to another area of flying, such as flight operations or aircraft maintenance, that doesn't require advanced math. As a result, many of them leave feeling they have more understanding about their career goals, even though they realize their ambition to fly might have been unrealistic. And those who aren't intimidated by the math requirements know that they're going to have to do a lot of work in that area to qualify.

I've also learned over the years how influential parents can be with their child's career plans. Many times children will steer toward a vocation, sometimes too early in life, because it seems to meet with approval at home. Announcing, "I'm planning on going pre-med" to friends and relatives is bound to bring handshakes and encouragement. All too often, children announce their plans and then feel obligated to carry through on what they "promised" rather than risk disappointing their parents. As a rule, it's better for parents to respond to announcements of career plans with the suggestion to *explore* careers rather than *choose* one; then children don't have to worry about losing face should they decide to overturn all their previous plans. It's become increasingly clear to me how important it is for parents to be supportive and encouraging during their child's various stages of career awareness and development. Inevitably, some young explorers will run up against unexpected information: educational requirements, performance standards, and other potential checks to their plans. Parents can help their children negotiate each of these through offering a consistent, yet realistic, belief in a successful outcome to the overall adventure of exploration. In order to be consistent, however, parents should know what to anticipate about the career development needs of young people, which is partly what this book is about. And second, so they can be realistic, parents should also be informed about the latest trends in education and the job market, which are also described in this book.

This book will tell you how to encourage your child to increase his or her options for finding challenging and rewarding career directions. The emphasis is on leading children to self-understanding in the area of career goals through education and experience. With humor, a minimum of jargon, and an emphasis on common sense, I'll show you that there's no mystery about helping children learn about career alternatives suitable for their interests and abilities—it's a matter of exploring alternatives. And I won't try to steer your child toward the "hot" careers for the next decade, either; instead I'll emphasize the importance of both academic and professional preparation in career planning. After all, hot jobs dry up in less than a decade, but a young person must prepare for a lifetime of career development. Each chapter in this book contributes to the overall theme that moving a child toward career choices is a step-by-step, exploratory process—slow for some, rapid for others. The ideas and suggestions I'll share with you will be appropriate to the developmental stages of children, beginning in midadolescence and continuing through the early years of college. Along the way, the accent will be on refining young people's ideas about the future while encouraging them to gradually assume more responsibility for their choices.

1

All About Career Planning

If a friend said, "Oh, we had a great time last year at Cape Cod—you should go," would you run off and begin making reservations? Probably not. You have your own vacation priorities: maybe sun, yes, but perhaps you would also want to do some mountain climbing, or be able to go to a concert every night. In other words, you know what you want, what you enjoy. You make your choice based on the results of previous vacations, what people tell you about their experiences, plus a little research on your own. You don't fly to a spot randomly chosen for you.

So it is with your child's career planning. There are four keys to successful career planning, each of them similar to what was just said about vacations. The four keys are:

Studying oneself
Becoming familiar with entry pathways to various occupations
Testing hypotheses and predictions about oneself in an occupation
Reviewing plans and progress with another person

These are the steps you will want to encourage your child to follow in exploring career interests and identifying future directions. Let's look at them one at a time.

Key 1: Studying Oneself

Notice that this first key isn't "Know thyself." Who does? As my father is fond of saying, life is a series of experiences, which is to say life is a series of steps in self-development. As a result of your child examining himself or herself from different viewpoints, you and your child will be able to discern a pattern that indicates career possibilities. Specifically, studying oneself means that your child should review or examine:

Background
Personality
Intelligence
Abilities
Likes
Dislikes
Wants
Expectations
Resources

The first half of this book is based on these factors. In Chapter 2, "How the Career Journey Begins," we'll talk about your child's background and how young people's values and beliefs develop over time. The next chapter, "A Closer Look at Your Child," focuses on personality, intelligence, and abilities. Chapter 4, "Helping to Explore Your Child's Interests," discusses the nature of career interest surveys and what these say about a person's occupational likes and dislikes.

By this point your child's self-study will be about completed and we'll next concentrate on the second aspect of successful career planning.

Key 2: Becoming Familiar with Entry Pathways to Various Occupations

"You can't get there from here," was the farmer's retort in an old gag about a city slicker who was lost in the country and asking for directions. In fact, most occupations are accessible only by certain routes.

Some of them can be shortcuts: a six-year college education in medicine leading to an M.D. degree. Some of them follow a well-traveled road: enlisting in the military under an apprenticeship program and continuing in the same field after discharge. And some of them are too risky to be worth recommending: for example, enrolling in a two-year nursing degree program despite predictions from nursing associations that a four-year degree is increasingly preferred.

The start of finding pathways to various careers begins with Chapter 5, "How Labor Market Trends Will Affect Your Child." One of the purposes of this chapter is to temper your child's expectations with a dose of factual information about what the future seems to hold: how the educational level of workers will continue to increase; how the service-producing industries are growing faster than goods-producing industries; and how employment projections portray the next decade and a half. This overview of the work world will give you and your child an understanding of general trends that affect the way we work and the kind of preparation your child needs to enter the work world.

Then it will be time for you and your child to get down to the business of becoming familiar with entry pathways to various occupations as described in Chapter 6, "How to Help Your Child Explore Careers." Step-by-step, the chapter explains the process of choosing occupations; ways of exploring occupations; sources of information about jobs and careers; and finally why your child might have difficulty in making career-related decisions. This is a common problem and the chapter concludes with some advice on helping your child with a decision-making plan.

Key 3: Testing Hypotheses and Predictions About Oneself in an Occupation

To understand what this key is about, imagine you're shopping for an item of clothing. Something looks appealing, so you think for an instant about how it would look on you. You do a quick evaluation of the style, your coloring, and the item's color. Based on your prediction of how it might look, you decide whether to actually try it on. Sometimes your hypothesis was correct and the item looks just as you hoped it would; sometimes there is an unexpected aspect or inconvenience that removes the piece from consideration and so you move on. Similarly when counseling students about choosing a college, I always encourage them to make campus visits. The analogy I like to use is that enrolling in a college without walking around the campus is like buying a used car without test-driving it.

An advanced step in career planning is trying out an occupation to see if it "fits." When it comes to the "fit" between young people and their hypotheses about certain careers there can be no real match without a test. So in Chapter 7, "Creative Ways for Your Child to Find Career Directions," I suggest that you encourage your child to take advantage of any of the following opportunities as ways to see whether an occupation or a career field feels comfortable:

Volunteer work

Job shadowing

Internships

Summer programs on college campuses

Youth exchange and study abroad programs

Like the student I mentioned in the introduction who thought she wanted to be a dietician but found she hated being in a kitchen, your child will either confirm his or her happiest notions about a career as a result of participating in one of these experiences, or will eliminate it as a possibility. In any case, your child will have gained important information and experience.

Suppose finances or circumstances prevent your child from using the suggestions described in Chapter 7. Then the following chapter, "Getting the Most Out of a First Job" will be helpful. Starting with a list of good jobs, only some of which require a high school diploma, and continuing with suggestions for finding work that's appropriate for high school students or younger children, the chapter emphasizes how almost any kind of work can be turned into an opportunity to test ideas about oneself and certain types of work. Take babysitting, for example. The novice babysitter who discovers that small children annoy him should think twice about occupations like teaching, childcare, camp counseling, and related fields. My experiences one summer working in a steel mill had this kind of result. On my last day, the foreman said to me, "Well, now you know how important it is that you get an education and not end up working in a steel mill." And it was true! Working in that hot, deafening environment gave me some career direction in a hurry. On the other hand, a first job may turn out to be the door to a real career.

The final chapter, "Opportunities for Self-Knowledge Through Additional Education," takes the long view that some young people need to take course work in occupational areas that interest them before they can make a firm career decision. This is not only a good idea, but critical in some instances where the education leading to the career is very demanding. Many engineering schools, for instance, require freshmen and sophomores to take some engineering classes right away so that they don't bide their time until junior year wondering whether engineering was the right choice. At the end of the chapter is a summary of what two-year and four-year colleges and universities can offer your child in the way of career planning. The Appendix includes an extensive list of resources that can provide you and your child with additional information about particular occupations or career fields in general. Most of the information is free or available at your local library.

The fourth key to successful career planning—your child's need to review plans and progress with another person—is the aspect of career planning that has a lot to do with you.

Key 4: Reviewing Plans and Progress with Another Person

Throughout the book I'm going to be relying on you to be your child's good listener and cheerleader. This means that to help your child explore careers, you should focus on what he or she says and offer encouragement. Naturally, because you love your child this shouldn't be difficult. I'm more concerned, however, about two things you should *not* do. The first is rooted in the "Here, let me do it for you" school of parenting. Mom or Dad takes over and runs the entire show. Here's an example.

A few months ago, a parent whose son was making no college or career plans called me. The boy, Josh, was generally unmotivated as far as school was concerned and was seeing a therapist. The therapist suggested that Josh consider a college far away where he would be on his own. Josh's dad was simply calling me to ask whether I would call Josh in and help him clarify his ideas about what he might like to study. I said I would, and Josh and I went to work a few days later. A month passed, and Josh's dad called me again. He said he'd made up his mind: Josh was going to go to a local college in the city and live at home, that way he could keep an eye on him. I asked whether Josh's therapist agreed. The dad said the therapist was out of the picture: in the dad's opinion, they weren't making any progress. (Can you see why the therapist recommended that Josh go far away and be on his own?) Josh's dad was crowding his son, stealing his turf, and not letting him make any independent decisions. Josh, in response, was digging his heels in and saying, "I'm not going to let you push me around."

Try not to take over the process of exploring careers for your child. If the child senses that you have a hidden agenda, that you really want him or her to be an actor instead of a chemist, then you will appear manipulative and the child will lose interest. And you will lose patience.

The second thing I hope you won't do is at the other extreme: to throw up your hands and say, "It's your life—you do it." At first glance, this might seem like not such a bad idea. After all, teachers and counselors (myself included) tell parents to gradually shift the responsibility for major decisions to their children. "Put the ball in your child's court," we tell you. But the accent is on *gradually*. Psychologically and physiologically, human beings respond best to challenges in which the stakes are raised gradually (think about your own experiences in connection with crash diets versus regular exercise and moderate dieting).

Let your child do more and more of the work related to career exploring. An example would be to show your child where in the Yellow Pages to look for clothing stores to work at. Then suggest that he make up a list of addresses. Next, help him put together a résumé, but make it clear that he will have to mail or deliver it himself and call for an appointment with the manager. In other words, all you do is some coaching; you don't go out and land your child a job. There will be times, of course, when your son or daughter will dawdle about something and then you'll be tempted to absent yourself from the whole situation, but remember that if you quit, you'll be setting a poor example.

I started out by saying that reviewing your child's plans and progress will require you to be a good listener and a cheerleader. Let's talk about good listening techniques, ones that will empower your child with a sense of "I know what I want—I can do it."

Being a Good Listener

At first, it might seem hard to believe that listening well will help anyone *do* something. We think of listening as a passive activity—sitting quietly while someone else does the work. But listening is a form of participation, and how well or poorly you listen has an effect on the person talking.

Think about this: Have you ever tried to explain a personal problem to a friend and realized that the friend wasn't really paying attention? Your initial feeling was probably discouragement, then perhaps you doubted whether the problem was important after all. But no, it *was* important, so you began to feel some anger at your friend for not caring. The point is that you felt uncertain and nothing was accomplished about solving the problem. It's not enough to just "let someone get it off his chest" unless you're an *active listener.* Active listening takes a little work, much as if someone says to you, "Can you give me a hand with this?" The person is asking you to participate and provide help. You don't need to have a degree in guidance or counseling to be an active listener; you only need to be familiar with and practice these tools: *acceptance, clarification,* and *probing.*

Acceptance

Acceptance merely means that you recognize that a person is coming to you with a concern and wants you to listen. Obviously, you can cut anyone off almost instantly and indicate that you don't accept the invitation to listen by shrugging your shoulders or saying, "Hmmm, how about that?"

Acceptance can be easily demonstrated by smiling, nodding your head, or saying things like, "I understand" or "I see." Once it's been established that you're giving your attention to the person, then you can move to the second step and begin lending a hand.

Clarification

Helping someone clarify her thinking can be done by either *restating* what she's saying or *paraphrasing* it. Restatement means repeating what the person has said using as many of the same words as possible. Paraphrasing is restating in your own words what the person's remarks mean to you. In neither case should you point out examples of illogical thinking, or offer your own insights; that only adds to the person's confusion. Here's an example:

> *Child:* Mom, I stayed up until 3 a.m. finishing that paper and now I'm too tired to get up. Can't I go in at noon? The paper's not due until last period.

You: You're too tired to go to school (restatement). But if you miss all your morning classes, you'll get behind (now a new problem has been introduced).

What you're aiming for when you help people clarify their thinking is *self-discovery.* People remember and act on things they've realized themselves. It gives them a sense of having control over the situation. And they'll feel more commitment to any solutions they come to on their own. Telling people what to do is sometimes effective in the short run (most of us fall into the habit of parenting by telling children what to do). But in the long run, most children demonstrate more and more reluctance to carry out solutions that have been imposed on them. Here's a better response to the situation above:

You: You're too tired to go to school (restatement). So you're asking whether you can skip your morning classes (paraphrase).

So far Mom has neither offered advice nor arrived at a decision. But the paraphrase is going to lead to continued discussion with the child, not Mom, doing most of the thinking.

Child: Right . . . I'm supposed to see a movie in Western Civ, though. We're going to have a quiz on it. Boy, I don't know.

At this point, it would be a good idea to do some *probing.*

Probing

Probing means asking a question that narrows the scope of the person's thinking. An open-ended probe encourages a person to focus on a general train of thought, as in asking, "Well, what do you think?" A directed probe attempts to focus on one topic, as in, "So if you miss the movie, then what?"

Child: If I miss the movie I'll have to see it after school and I can't because I've got practice all week. Oh, forget it—it's not worth staying home. I'll just be tired, I guess.

Now let's put acceptance, clarification, and probing together in a different situation, one that's career-related:

You: Did you pick up a copy of your career interest survey at school? What did it say?

Child: Not much. It said I wasn't good at anything.

You: The interest survey said you're not good at anything. (restatement)

Child: Well, not that I'm not *good* at anything. It just said I'm not interested in much.

You: What did it say you're interested in exactly? (directed probe)

Child: Regulations enforcement and management. That's it—those were the two highest. That's all I get to pick from.

You: You're bothered because there weren't more, is that right? (paraphrase)

Child: Yeah, I was hoping there'd be a lot to pick from.

You: Why?

Child: Well, I don't know. Just seems like regulations enforcement and management isn't much, that's all.

You: What is regulations enforcement? (directed probe)

Child: I don't even know.

You: How can you find out? (directed probe)

Child: See my counselor I guess. Maybe he'll explain it to me.

You: What do you think? Sound like a good idea? (open-ended probe)

Child: Yeah, I'll go in there tomorrow and make an appointment.

Obviously, the child hasn't arrived at his ideal job in life, but he has moved off the idea that finding out about his interests is futile and his parent avoided telling him what to do.

We'll be using these listening strategies at points throughout the book and eventually you'll feel confident about using them.

Being Your Child's Cheerleader

In addition to being a good listener, being a cheerleader should be your second contribution to your child's career planning. The role of a cheerleader is to express optimism. This doesn't mean being unrealistic or suggesting alternatives that are unrealistic. On the contrary, being a cheerleader means reducing anxiety about the future—the way professional cheerleaders do about the outcome of the game—and emphasizing possible alternatives.

Your biggest opponent will be your child's skepticism. From my experiences as a teacher and a counselor I've learned that skepticism is the religion of young people. They are at a point when the idealism of childhood is being tempered by an appreciation that the world isn't perfect. Hence, most young people tend to go a bit overboard and accept little on faith; being caught unaware or seeming gullible just isn't cool.

So your son or daughter may meet your enthusiasm about some career possibility with body language—crossed arms, ironic expression, look of impatience—that can be frustrating. Or she may drag her feet about meeting some goal that you and she have set, such as checking out a book from the library on a certain occupation. Actually, some of this skepticism may be founded on anxiety about the future. Experts have learned that senior-itis among high school students is quite often separation anxiety: high school is ending, friendships are breaking apart, and the future looms dark and secret on the horizon. Young people can be this way about career planning, too. Often *they're more worried about what they can't do than what they can.* I've had students come into my office more to confirm their worst fears than anything else: "I got a C in trigonometry this quarter, so I guess that's it for me and the Air Force Academy, right?"

You can do a lot to diffuse your child's anxiety about the future by emphasizing alternatives. Young people tend to see things in black-and-white: either I'm popular or I'm not; either I keep my mouth shut or everybody will think I'm stupid. When it comes to careers, young people extend this attitude to the work world: if I go to college, I'll be a winner and successful; if I don't, I'll be a loser my whole life.

Continue to counter black-and-white thinking with optimism and an insistence on alternatives. Especially in the work world, doors leading to careers don't slam shut with a thud forever on hapless seekers. There are many avenues leading to vocational success.

2

How the Career Journey Begins

What's the first step in a child's career journey? How about the question, "What do you want to be when you grow up?" It's a sort of catechism: children are asked this, adults wait, and then come the expected responses: A fireman! A nurse! A teacher! All are greeted with approval or expressions of surprise and admiration. But isn't it interesting that chidren usually have an answer ready? This seems to indicate that their thinking about "what to be" has started earlier. How early? Why do they select what they do? And why are certain choices the most popular?

Small Children and Pretend Work

Small children notice that grown-ups work. One little girl was asked what her father does for a living. She said, "He flies airplanes." Actually, her dad was a businessman, but the child and her mother took him to the airport so often that the child assumed he was a pilot.

Small children also notice that work is important. For example, the parting explanation that parents often give children as they drop them

11

off for day care is, "Daddy has to go to work now, so you stay here and I'll see you later." Or in other situations, the question, "Where's Mommy?" brings the reply, "She's at work—she'll be here when it gets dark." Children conclude that whatever work is, it must be compelling.

So when children play and create their scenarios with dolls and figurines that live exciting lives, going to work is often an activity that gets scripted in. "Goodbye, I'm going to work now!" says the doll and off it goes. But where is it going, and what does it do there? The doll is probably a doctor, a policewoman, a mail carrier, or some other easily differentiated worker. After all, these people perform tasks that are understandable; they put out fires, make people well, grow food, drive trucks—all things where the tasks and the results are apparent. In addition, helping professions are probably the most popular among children because they like to join in and contribute. Consequently, doing praiseworthy, constructive work like building houses satisfies their desire to participate in positive ways. The number of professions children choose from is also limited to what they've seen: teachers, day care workers, cooks, and others within the range of their experience.

Preadolescence

By the time children are in the fourth through eighth grades they are aware of being "good at" some things. They don't expect every drawing or piece of homework to be put on the refrigerator any longer. They recognize differences in quality and achievement; they cheer loudest when the best hitter in their class gets up to bat. They beam when there's a contest—a spelling bee, an election, or a hobby fair—and they win.

Achievements bring attention and status, and this is a time when children begin splitting off down broad career paths that lure them by the promise of still more praise. The child who consistently does well in arithmetic wants to extend his record indefinitely. As you can imagine, it's important that each child feel the spotlight of success as an inducement to keep trying. Some parents wonder how to encourage a child who is "just average." The answer is to expose the child to more opportunities through clubs, teams, lessons, and camps. Then once the child discovers an activity he excels at and enjoys, give him room to "jump in with both feet," as Leonard Bernstein once recommended for finding a vocation in life.

Preadolescence is also the time when children begin to recognize the value of money. An allowance, given for work outside routine household chores, is a good way to introduce a child to simple principles of money management. Even better, jobs outside the home, such as a paper route, lawn mowing, and babysitting, give children glimpses of employers' expectations—responsible behavior, punctuality, honesty— and a notion of what good workers are paid for.

Through these fundamental experiences—receiving praise for their achievements, working and earning pocket money—preadolescents begin to express preferences for certain kinds of activities.

Adolescence

Now we come to where childhood and adulthood intersect: adolescence. I once heard someone say that adolescence is the closest any of us get to psychosis. Sound extreme? A social worker friend of mine put it this way: "At 12 years old, your child is like a round, smooth, glass ball. You look at your son or daughter and say to yourself, 'What a great job I've done.' And then that glass ball drops, shatters into a hundred pieces, and your child will spend the rest of his adolescence and probably a good part of his young adulthood trying to fit the pieces together again."

What happens is that a number of normal developmental changes come so quickly that children are hurled from childhood to the threshold of adulthood in just a few years. They are like passengers on a rocket sled—the acceleration exerts pressure on their bodies and powerful influences on their minds. Here's a summary of important challenges and changes that occur during adolescence.

Coping with physical growth and development. A husky high school freshman told me that one day he stepped on the scale at home and weighed 135 pounds. The next time he weighed himself, he was 2 inches taller and 25 pounds heavier. Imagine experiencing such dramatic differences as adults—we'd think we were losing control of our bodies! The impact on young people is especially acute since they are already sensitive about their appearance; hence, a youngster getting ready to go out for the evening rummages through half his wardrobe trying to adorn a physique he's hardly acquainted with. The result can be a shirt that pulls at the buttons, and pants that are long enough but too tight in the waist, bringing wails of frustration and disgust. (I know one teenage boy who is convinced that his mother is deliberately putting his clothes in a hot dryer and shrinking them.)

Becoming less dependent. Teenagers can't wait to try their wings: every day, hundreds of 15-year-olds with temporary driving permits navigate to the store in the family car for a gallon of milk. How else are they supposed to ease into independence without opportunities to practice it? On the flip side, teenagers don't ask every time they want to make a bid for freedom—they just do it. For example, a girl tells her parents she's going to a friend's house and ends up at a drive-through hamburger place because that's where the popular kids go. But if you press her about *why* she wants to go there, she couldn't say; it's just got something to do with scaling the confining walls of home and breaking out into the open.

Turning to peers for status and recognition. I had a friend in high school whose grades started to drop in junior year. By summer, he was showing no interest in going to college. One night, his dad gave me a lift home. On the way he said, "Talk to Jerry about going to college, will you? You and Jack are his best friends and maybe you can persuade him." I was humbled by how a grown-up was giving me the kind of authority reserved for parents. But most parents come to realize (and usually with chagrin) that their teenagers put more credence in what their friends do and say than what their parents stand for. An especially tough situation for parents is when a child travels in a crowd that scoffs at traditional notions of success. The whole edifice of conduct at school, grades, career and college plans can be jeopardized. In this case, the best thing to do is either be patient and ride the situation out, or if the behavior of the group is dangerous, make major changes in the child's life with the help of professional advice.

Using enhanced intellectual powers. Teenagers are generally argumentative. They disagree loudly with each other and tend to be skeptical of people's motives. The technique they employ the most is pure sophistry, reducing an issue to the point where further discussion becomes purposeless: "What do you mean 'responsible'? You mean I can't be trusted to dress myself—is that what you mean by 'responsible'?" Actually, this attitude is a good sign. We don't want young people to attend school for thirteen years and come out passive thinkers. On the other hand, their predilection to take everything with a grain of salt can be tiresome.

The most effective parry you can offer is this: Check it out for yourself. Discourage generalizations and the hardening of biases by encouraging your child to take creative risks and find out what might be on the other side of questions and problems. Say, for example, your son is convinced he can't cook. Guide him through making a meal and rave about the outcome. Or maybe your daughter thinks it "gross" for a woman to be in love with a younger man. Find a couple of articles at the library on this topic and show them to her—not with the intent to prove her wrong, but to make clear people's reasons.

In a world—and especially a nation like ours—where values are constantly being scrutinized, a trait worth nurturing in your child is openmindedness. Otherwise, he or she could fall into the habit of paying lip service to ideals and opinions that are really just a patchwork of indefensible prejudices.

Testing values learned as a child. By the time children are adolescents they are familiar with all kinds of values—ones they've been taught and ones they've seen demonstrated. Gradually, they have to sift through them and reject ones they don't feel are worthwhile. But how do they do this? Think for a moment about how you decide to eliminate pieces of clothing or things from the basement. You probably evaluate each item in terms of its usefulness and practicality. Teenagers do the same thing as they sort through their values, choose some, and gradually weave a network of beliefs. Unfortunately, values concerning sexual behavior, honesty, and other important matters are not the same as rusty tools in the basement; tossing out some values can have significant consequences. Countless arguments at the dinner table have their roots in conflicts over the values parents want their children to adopt, and children's reluctance to accept them. (The issue of independence is involved here, too.)

Realize, however, that often children are just testing: "You say I should act or think a certain way, but why?" Once again, their curiosity deserves a respectful response, not a put-down. But since ethical questions are usually pretty knotty anyway, this is a juncture when *deeds* on your part would be more influential than *words* alone. You can think of hypothetical situations to prove your point until you're blue in the face, but as a counselor and a parent, I've found that being an example of having certain values is very persuasive. Even if you can think of times in your life that have illustrated what *not* to do, the point is clear. Children are usually impressed by adults' experiences: demonstrate the values you want your children to have and share your experiences with your children so that they will have your example to draw on as they attempt to forge their own beliefs.

These are some of the key developmental changes that adolescents face. Now let's really put the pressure on them and begin asking them the same question we asked ten years earlier: What do you want to be? Only this time, teenagers realize that very soon they will indeed have to "do something" with their lives.

The Pressure to "Do Something"

We love our children and we want them to succeed. Part of our vision of their future probably includes several hallmarks of security and stability: a house, a family, and that foggy notion of a "good job." What does this picture really add up to? Independence. As Kahlil Gibran wrote, "Your children are not yours." The goal of childraising is to prepare children to be free. However, real independence intimidates many young people. They yearn for it, but they worry about it, too, because freedom is risky.

Choosing a vocation is a big step on the road to independence. Consequently, some children will hang back, loathe to do anything that will saw away at the bonds tying them to their family. In fact, putting off making occupational decisions increases children's dependency. With nothing but pocket money, no prospects, and no clear ambitions, a teenager can remain poised on the edge of childhood as long as he likes. If he continues to go from one dead-end job to another long enough, eventually he will become a fixture in the family home and his aging parents will come to depend on him. Childhood stretches into a lifetime.

Helping a child move ahead with vocational plans is a part of parenting that comes late in a child's development. But that doesn't mean your influence as a parent has dwindled to nothing. Studies show parents, not friends or teachers, have the most influence over children's college and career plans. Parents can have more impact on children's career plans than even grades or academic abilities do. Let's use a negative example. I know a girl who was in the top 15 percent in a class of 600. Her Scholastic Aptitude Test (SAT) scores put her at the 92d percentile nationwide. But she went to a nearby college that was much too easy for her. She enrolled there because, in her father's words, "It was good enough for your mother and me and it's good enough for you."

I'm assuming that's not your attitude, that you want your child to reach as high as she can. Here is what you can do.

Encourage self-direction in your child. To understand my point about the importance of self-direction and career choice, take a moment to rank the following jobs in the order of prestige you would assign them:

_____ Lawyer	_____ Barber
_____ Physician	_____ Farmer
_____ Bricklayer	_____ Machinist
_____ School superintendent	_____ Secretary
_____ Civil engineer	_____ Plumber
_____ Janitor	_____ Salesperson
_____ Army captain	_____ Electrician
_____ Coal miner	_____ Computer programmer
_____ Truck driver	_____ Insurance agent
_____ Elementary school teacher	_____ Banker

Most likely the jobs you ranked as having the least prestige were ones that require the least self-direction. In other words, jobs where workers are told what to do and fulfill the tasks as instructed rank far down the list.

If you want your child to aim for careers that society esteems, ones for which creativity and self-reliance are rewarded with better-than-average pay, begin teaching self-direction. Let your child plan activities that will challenge his or her ability to follow directions and make decisions: taking the bus into the city for a movie; flying out to visit a relative for two weeks in the summer; taking a part-time job working exclusively with grownups. This will prepare the child for greater responsibilities in the work world and he'll know through experience that he's equal to them. Insistence on conformity, on the other hand, or "do-as-I-say" parenting will lay the groundwork for low-prestige jobs requiring little independence of mind.

Stay informed about your child's progress at school. Level of education still has a lot to do with lifetime earnings. Here are some statistics from Ernest Boyer's *College: The Undergraduate Experience in America:*

Average total lifetime earnings by education and sex:

Female high school graduate: $381,000
Female college graduate: $523,000
Male high school graduate: $861,000
Male college graduate: $1,190,000

The curriculums of high schools are usually divided into *vocational education* and *general education,* or *college preparatory.* Considering the rate at which technology is changing the way we work and what's required of workers, I recommend that your child be enrolled mainly in college preparatory classes. Ideally, at the end of four years of high school, he or she should have completed:

• Four years of English
• Three years of mathematics
• Two years of social studies
• Two years of laboratory sciences
• Two years of foreign language

If your child is attracted to vocational classes, suggest that they be taken as electives.

Encourage your daughter to take a wide range of courses and get involved in extracurricular activities. In looking at those figures about lifetime earnings, did you notice the disparity between what men and women earn? Some sociologists argue that the income gap has its origins in the classroom. Girls often take fewer math and science courses than boys, precluding careers in engineering, medicine, and other fields. Don't let doors close quietly but firmly for your daughter even before she graduates from high school. Recommend that she enroll in that third year of math. Some girls substitute a general science course—earth or space science, for instance—for a laboratory course in chemistry or biology. This is a shortcut, too, and I don't recommend it.

Another behavior seen in high school girls, one that teachers inadvertently reinforce, is passivity in the classroom. Girls who do their work well and don't argue with the teacher are often pointed out as good students. Careers demanding assertiveness—law, business, and many others—may seem too rough and tumble for anyone whose reputation in school has been founded on obliging behavior. While you can't keep tabs on the atmosphere of all your daughter's classes, extracurricular activities can provide practice at competition and leadership. Your child can choose from any of these categories:

School management: Student councils, cabinets, safety patrols, monitors, assistants, and class officers

Religious and social welfare: Hi-Y, Boy Scouts, Girl Scouts, Big Brother or Big Sister, Junior Red Cross, and candystripers at the local hospital

School publications: Newspapers, magazines, yearbooks, and handbooks

Social events: Parties, dances, mixers, picnics, dinners, and banquets

Special interest clubs: Photography, radio, mathematics, film, foreign language, etc.

Dramatics and public speaking: Plays, debates, and speech contests

Music activities: Chorus, glee club, quartets, and operettas

Athletics: Football, basketball, baseball, tennis, swimming, golf, track, and field hockey.

Find out about sources of career information in your community. Chapter 6 describes the various types of occupational information available in most libraries and schools, but don't overlook the following resources, either:

Placement offices in trade and technical schools

Career planning and placement offices in colleges

Job Service offices affiliated with the U.S. Employment Service

Vocational rehabilitation agencies

Counseling services offered by community organizations

Commercial firms and professional consultants

The professionals at these organizations would be happy to help you and your child with his or her career journey.

A child's awareness of careers and vocational preferences does grow step-by-step, and you can be instrumental in assisting that development. So far we've been speaking in general terms about young people; now let's narrow our field of vision and talk just about your son's or daughter's personality and abilities.

3

A Closer Look
At Your Child

Your child's personality is complex. There are over 18,000 words in English to describe the way a person thinks, feels, and acts. And even though you might be able to summarize your child's personality in a few words such as outgoing, pleasant, even-tempered, the nature of personality by definition—*all of the ways a person reacts to his or her environment*—isn't simple. In fact, I once heard a psychologist remark that personality is the "deepest trance of all," meaning, I suppose, that most of our subconscious motives for behaving the way we do are unknown even to ourselves.

For a long time, people have tried to understand personality by categorizing it into types. Hippocrates, the Greek physician, described four types of personality according to the balance among four body fluids. Another ancient observer of behavior, Theophrastus, proposed "characterology," a study of human beings based on thirty extreme types. In our own century, Swiss psychiatrist Carl G. Jung suggested two broad personality types: introverts and extroverts, terms that are sometimes overused. According to Jung, introverts are concerned with their own thoughts and impressions; extroverts, on the other hand, prefer objective information and participating in activities. From this, there's a tendency to label creative people introverts and "team players" extroverts. Jung said, however, that in his view everyone has traits of both types. Recently, the terms Type A and Type B have been introduced to cover all kinds of behavior. According to the theory, Type A people are compulsively hard workers, and this compulsion can lead to health problems. Type B people are more relaxed and less likely to suffer from stress-related illnesses.

As you read these descriptions, perhaps you are thinking, "Is my child like this?" just as when reading lists of symptoms associated with diseases we often think "Hey, I've had that!" But generalizing about children and their behavior has as many pitfalls as diagnosing the condition of our health from a textbook: there are too many variables or *traits* that make a difference. As I said, children's personalities— anyone's personality—is complex.

But let's at least make an attempt at understanding why children behave as they do, and prefer certain kinds of activities over others, by looking at how personality develops.

The Parts That Add Up to Personality

Children are born with dispositions. This might sound like a cop-out. After all, saying that "He's just that way," is not exactly scientific. But you know from your own experience that even when your son or daughter was tiny, he or she had the rudiments of a personality that could not have been acquired in the first few weeks of life. The disposition arrived intact: the child acted fussy or quiet or active, for instance, from the start. (Being "born that way" reminds me of the time I overheard a woman ask a little boy, "Where'd you get those beautiful eyes?" He shrugged. "I dunno. They came with my head.")

Children are born with physical traits that indirectly affect personality: the undersized boy who compensates by being assertive; the pretty girl who feels comfortable in social situations because she draws attention. Our intuitive understanding is so strong about how physical traits affect personality that even in literature, authors will sometimes give characters a pronounced physical trait, such as Philip Carey's clubfoot in *Of Human Bondage,* to help us know the character better. It's not that physical characteristics by themselves are so important, but that social factors compel us to act certain ways based partly on our appearance.

One of the most important social factors—a child's home environment—shapes personality too. From my viewpoint as a teacher, for example, I've seen that kids who are organized and get good grades almost always come from homes where those values are encouraged. I've had students of average intelligence do well in high-powered classes because they're always prepared and their outlook is positive, and I've had bright students in remedial classes who are there because they're directionless and lacking in self-esteem. The notion that there are smart kids and dumb kids ignores the major impact children's upbringing has on their attitude, behavior, and personality in general.

On another level of home life, a child's relationship to brothers, sisters, and parents also conditions personality. Studies of the relationship between a child's birth-order position in the family and his or her behavior are inconclusive, but every parent knows that younger children seek to imitate, and surpass if they can, their older siblings. How this striving for superiority is greeted, especially by parents, whether with praise or disapproval, is important. In fact, in most endeavors, the audience that children are playing to is their parents; parents who give time to learning about their children's achievements and setbacks send a signal to the children that they are valued and their efforts are worthwhile. How well they perform will become important to them, and this is the basis of a winning attitude.

Finally, a child's friends influence his or her personality. Friends are the people a child "works" with and, just as in the adult world of work, you can only be as good as the people you work with. Groups of friends and companions behave in ways that reflect their values. High school students can instantly categorize each other by the groups they belong to: "He's on the football team" (competitive, athletic); "She's in Spanish National Honor Society" (brainy, enjoys school); "He's in student government" (ambitious, believes in the system). Of course, this kind of labeling goes against our ideals of wanting to be open-minded about other people, but even in our own neighborhood we ask each other, "What's he do for a living?" and try to deduce all sorts of things about the person from the reply. Likewise, what friends a child has are not only a statement of what's important to her or him, but also an indirect insight into the child's personality.

Why Does My Child Act That Way?

Having described some of the factors that contribute to children's personalities, let's move on to seeing how personality is expressed through behavior.

A friend of mine was a little concerned recently when her 13-year-old son came hurrying downstairs with a couple of superhero dolls he'd been given at age 7. "They're going to have a fight!" he announced, and he turned the coffee table into a wrestling mat where the plastic enemies went at it for 15 minutes. My friend asked, "Do you think it's OK for a teenager to be playing like that?"

Emotional maturity doesn't develop at an even, predictable pace. Not all children are ready for kindergarten at age 5; not all teenagers are ready to date at 15. Once again, personality differences move the milemarkers of maturity around for everyone. The 15-year-old may be too shy about dating, yet not uninterested in having a boyfriend or girlfriend. Getting back to my friend's son, he wasn't regressing by pretending with dolls; maybe he had just rediscovered two favorite toys and wanted to re-experience the fun he used to have playing with them. As it turns out, he hasn't played with them since, so it's likely other, more typical 13-year-old interests have replaced the superheroes and returned them to the toy box for good.

An important behavior influencer is self-concept. Self-concept is the sum of a person's thoughts about how he thinks others see him and what he thinks about himself. Many of the personality disorders that professionals see in clients have their origins in inappropriate self-concepts: the woman who's convinced she isn't lovable; the man whose self-worth is tied to his father's opinion of him. People who spend a lot of time with children—teachers, counselors, social workers—learn to watch for behavior clues to self-concept: slouching and mumbling, for example, versus making direct eye contact and moving energetically. Although personality has a lot to do with a person's suitability for certain careers, in the long run, self-concept is a more important factor in leading a young person in one career direction or another. Other key factors are *interest, ability, aptitude,* and *intelligence.*

What Can My Child Do?

In Chapter 4, we'll pinpoint some of your child's *interests,* which are generally an outgrowth of likes and dislikes. In career planning, there's usually a connection between the experiences a person has had in connection with an activity and his or her interest in doing it regularly. A teenager who has spent many happy hours assembling electronic kits would probably express interest in all types of work involving technology, repair, and fine work.

Interests are also tempered by the amount of *ability* a person can bring to bear on a task. "Oh, I hate math," is a waiver many people use to express their lack of interest in anything involving numbers because they haven't acquired the ability. Abilities are learned skills; tests that measure abilities only highlight a person's present abilities, ones they have learned. No test has yet been devised that measures innate, undiscovered abilities. On the other hand, people who hate math may not have the *aptitude* for it, either. In other words, their ability in math is limited by their facility at learning math. In ordinary language, we might say the person doesn't have a knack for picking up math (though this is an oversimplification—a series of poor teachers, or not recognizing how math is useful may be the underlying reason). Unfortunately, there is little agreement on what *intelligence* is, though that doesn't dissuade people from testing it or comparing the results. Many experts say that a person's level of intelligence stays the same throughout life. This might sound like a significant predictor of intellectual and/or financial achievement in life, but a person's other traits—creativity or lack of it, amount of ambition, and as discussed earlier, self-concept—end up counting as much as intelligence in a person's life. MENSA, an organization for people considered to have superior intelligence based on IQ level, has members in virtually all economic brackets whose work ranges from theoretical physics to manual labor. (If your child is gifted, a book worth getting is Fenton Keyes' *Exploring Careers for the Gifted*. New York: Rosen, 1985.)

How You Can Help

Any of the aspects we've discussed so far—self-concept, interest, ability, aptitude, and intelligence—can be tested, and I'll explain how in the next chapter. But here are some things you can do right now to help your child begin thinking about careers.

Look for patterns and accentuate the positive. A friend of the family could go into your child's bedroom right now and see signs of your son's or daughter's interests: model airplanes, posters of movie stars, a rock collection, an aquarium, books of poetry, sports equipment, a stamp collection, watercolor pictures taped to the wall—a museum your child has built to his or her interests and achievements. Take a few steps back from your child, like a friend of the family, and look for the "big picture" your child presents. One obvious place to start is school. Many career planning surveys ask respondents to list their favorite subjects in school. In which subjects has your child performed the best? To give you an idea of how ability in certain academic areas can lead to careers, the following chart shows careers grouped by school subject. This information was current as of 1986. (The DOT number refers to the *Dictionary of Occupational Titles* published every other year by the U.S. Bureau of Labor Statistics. This reference book, available in most public libraries, gives detailed descriptions of these occupations.)

English

Occupation	DOT Number	Outlook	Average Initial Salary
Advertising Manager	164.117-010	Good	$20,500
Columnist/Commentator	131.067-010	Fair	$16,800
Creative Director	141.067-010	Fair	$18,300
Director, Radio and TV	159.067-014	Fair	Unavailable
Disk Jockey	159.147-014	Good	$13,700
Editor, Newspaper	132.017-014	Fair	$23,700
Editorial Assistant	132.267-014	Fair	$13,700
Newswriter	131.267-014	Good	$20,100
Photojournalist	143.062-034	Fair	$17,500
Proofreader	209.387-030	Good	$12,800
Public Relations Worker	165.067-010	Good	$27,000
Writer, Fiction/Nonfiction	131.067-046	Fair	$15,000
Writer, Screen	131.087-018	Poor	$11,900
Writer, Technical	131.267-026	Good	$21,800

Foreign Language

Occupation	DOT Number	Outlook	Average Initial Salary
Chef	187.161-010	Good	$18,000
Customs Official	168.267.022	Good	$16,000
Historic Site Supervisor	102.117-010	Good	$19,000
Import/Export Agent	184.117-022	Good	$21,000
Intelligence Expert	059.267-010	Good	$22,000
Public Relations Specialist	165.067-010	Good	$17,000
Travel Agent	225.157-010	Good	$16,000
Translator	137.267-010	Good	$20,000

Fine Arts

Occupation	DOT Number	Outlook	Average Initial Salary
Actor	150.047-010	Poor	$ 5,000
Artist, Commercial	141.081-014	Good	$17,000
Designer, Fashion	142.061-018	Good	$14,100
Designer, Interior	142.051-014	Fair	$16,000
Fashion Merchandising	162.157-018	Good	$16,000
Illustrator	141.061-022	Good	$18,100
Make-up Artist	333.071-010	Fair	$14,000
Photographer	143.062-030	Fair	$18,000
Stage Director (Theater Production)	150.067-010	Good	$22,700

Math

Occupation	DOT Number	Outlook	Average Initial Salary
Actuary	020.167-010	Good	$18,000
Auditor	160.162-040	Good/Excellent	$17,000
Cartographer	018.261-026	Good	$20,000
Efficiency Engineer	012.167-070	Fair	$19,000
Financial Planner	026.167-014	Good	$22,000
Mathematician	020.067-014	Good	$18,000
Meteorologist	012.067-010	Fair/Good	$19,000
Psychometrician	045.067-018	Good	$21,000
Operations Research Analyst	020.067-018	Good	$17,000
Salary/Wage Administrator	166.167-022	Good/Fair	$18,000
Navigator	196.167-014	Fair	$22,000
Teacher	091.227-010	Good	$17,000
Computer Applications Engineer	020.062-010	Excellent	$27,000
Engineering Analyst	020.067-010	Excellent	$29,000
Statistician	620.067-022	Excellent	$22,000

Physical Education

Occupation	DOT Number	Outlook	Average Initial Salary
Athletic Director		Fair	$28,000
Athletic Trainer	153.224-010	Good/Excellent	$20,000

Occupation	DOT Number	Outlook	*Average* *Initial Salary*
Coach	153.227-010	Fair/Good	Varies
Exercise Specialist		Good/Fair	$18,000
Recreation Director	187.137-010	Good	$17,000
P.E. Teacher	091.227-010	Fair/Good	$20,000
Athletic Manager	153.117-010	Fair	Varies
Professional Scout	153.117-010	Poor	Varies

Science

Occupation	DOT Number	Outlook	*Average* *Initial Salary*
Anesthesiologist	070.101-010	Good	$100,000
Astronomer	021.067-010	Poor	$26,000
Audiologist	076.101-010	Good	$21,800
Biochemist	041.061-026	Very Good	$21,600
Biologist	041.061-030	Good/Fair	$25,400
Biologist, Marine	041.061-022	Good/Fair	$22,600
Botanist	041.061-038	Good/Fair	$21,700
Cardiologist	070.101-014	Good/Fair	$100,000
Chemist	022.061-010	Good/Fair	$22,800
Chiropractor	079.101-010	Fair	$30,000
Dairy Technologist	040.061-022	Fair	$20,700
Dentist	072.101-010	Poor	$60,000
Dermatologist	070.101-018	Good	$100,000
Dietician, Research	077.061-010	Fair	$18,600
Engineer, Biomedical	019.061-010	Good	$26,900
Entomologist	041.061-046	Poor	$17,200
General Practitioner	070.101-022	Fair	$76,400
Geneticist	041.061-050	Good	$20,000
Geologist	024.061-018	Fair	$24,900
Gynecologist	070.101-034	Good	$81,700
Microbiologist	041.061-058	Good	$20,000
Neurologist	070.101-050	Good	$100,000
Obstetrician	070.101-054	Very Good	$81,700
Ophthalmologist	070.101-058	Very Good	$100,000
Optometrist	079.101-018	Good	$29,700
Oral Pathologist	072.061-010	Good	$95,000
Oral Surgeon	072.101-018	Good	$95,000
Orthodontist	072.101-022	Good/Very Good	$95,000
Osteopathic Physician	071.101-010	Fair	Unavailable
Pathologist	070.061-010	Good	$100,000
Pediatrician	070.101-066	Very Good	$76,400

Occupation	DOT Number	Outlook	Average Initial Salary
Periodontist	072.101-030	Good/Very Good	$95,000
Pharmacist	074.161-010	Fair/Good	$29,100
Pharmacologist	041.061-074	Good	$22,500
Physicist	023.061-014	Poor	$25,900
Podiatrist	079.101-022	Fair/Good	$54,000
Psychiatrist	070.107-014	Very Good	$95,000
Speech Pathologist	076.107-010	Good	$21,800
Surgeon	070.101-094	Good	$100,000
Urologist	070.101-098	Good	$100,000
Veterinarian	073.101-010	Fair/Good	$22,000
Zoologist	041.061-090	Fair/Good	$21,800

Social Sciences

Occupation	DOT Number	Outlook	Average Initial Salary
Anthropologist	055.067-010	Fair	$24,000
Archeologist	055.067-018	Fair	$16,000
Archivist	101.167-010	Fair	$21,800
Caseworker, Child Welfare	195.107-014	Fair	$21,600
Clergy Member	120.007-010	Varies by faith	$25,000
Counselor	045.107-010	Good	$24,500
Curator	102.017-010	Fair	$19,600
Economist	050.067-010	Good	$21,500
Historian	052.067-022	Poor	$24,300
Home Economist	096.121-014	Good	$19,200
Lawyer	110.107-010	Poor	$30,200
Librarian	100.127-014	Poor	$20,200
Parole Officer	195.167-030	Good	$22,600
Political Scientist	051.067-010	Fair	$21,700
Professor	090.227-010	Poor	$25,500
Psychologist, Counseling	045.107-026	Good	$24,000
Social Worker	195.107-018	Good	$21,000
Sociologist	054.067-014	Fair	$26,900
Teacher, Elementary	092.227-010	Good/Excellent	$15,900
Teacher, Handicapped	094.227-018	Good	$16,800
Teacher, Preschool	092.227-018	Excellent	$15,900
Teacher, Secondary	091.227-010	Good	$15,900
Urban Planner	199.167-014	Poor	$27,000

If school has been hard for your child don't despair; it doesn't automatically follow that the road to finding the right career will also be rough. There's no doubt that good performance in school helps smooth the way to more opportunities, but consider this: in a 20-year follow-up study of children who took the Scholastic Aptitude Test, no significant correlation was found between the scores children received on the test and how they rated themselves in terms of happiness and success. In fact, the only relationship that seems to exist between school performance and later success was this: those students who were involved in extracurricular activities, both in and out of school, more often rated themselves as successful. In the long run, nonacademic interests and abilities were better predictors.

As you can see, whether your child's interests, abilities, and aptitudes are apparent in or out of school, there are plenty of avenues to careers worth exploring. In the next chapter, we'll find out more about your child's specific interests and all about resources you and your child can turn to for help with bringing your child's vocational future into focus.

4

Helping to Explore Your Child's Interests

"Organize your energies along your own line of natural interest and persistence, and you will do more, much more, so much better."

Georg Kaiser

Interests are closely linked to likes and dislikes. And when it comes to career planning, people's vocational interests are usually tied to the experiences they've had participating in various activities. You might enjoy cooking, for example, because you associate it with taking care of your family, happy occasions, or doing something creative. You might not like cooking for reasons just as simple: it's time consuming, requires concentration, and involves a slight element of risk—will they like what you make? But if you enjoy cooking, you're probably pretty good at it because you take the time to follow the recipe and you've acquired skills the indifferent cook doesn't care to learn. There's no secret about it, really; as the quote above points out, putting your energies into work you enjoy will result in more finished work and better quality work, too.

Regrettably, according to the U.S. Department of Labor, *75 percent* of Americans say they don't like their jobs. That means most Americans go off to work reluctantly, maybe resentfully; work is drudgery. And guess on which day of the week most American men have heart attacks? Monday morning. Apparently the thought of what lies ahead at work literally kills them.

The purpose of this book is to avoid such a grim scenario for today's young people, whose future stretches before them. Let's open as many doors as possible before all sorts of obligations—family, financial, and personal—restrict choices. Start by finding out what your child is really interested in.

Exploring Vocational Interests

A vocational interest survey is not a test; there is no failing score, nor should the results be used to make academic predictions. The results are intended to tell your child whether his or her interests are similar to those of successful men and women in a particular field. If they are, then chances are excellent that he or she will like the people and the work. Keep in mind, however, that this won't guarantee success. Whether your child has the *abilities* and *aptitudes* for the work is important, too. But interest surveys provide occupational leads worth pursuing.

Here's a rundown of some of the most widely administered interest surveys, all of which can be given by a school counselor, or by counseling services. Whenever your child takes a survey or a test, it's a good idea to make an appointment to discuss the results with a professional.

Kuder Occupational Interest Survey—Form DD: Grade 11 through Adult. The Kuder Survey gives an indication of a person's interests in 10 broad interest areas: outdoor, mechanical, computational, scientific, persuasive, artistic, literary, musical, social service, and clerical. Items on this inventory are grouped in 100 clusters of 3:

Direct an orchestra	( )	( )	( )
Compose music	( )	( )	( )
Repair musical instruments	( )	( )	( )

Students must select from the three items the activity they would prefer to do the most and the one they would prefer to do least. On the score report sheet, students' responses are shown on 126 occupational scales and 48 college major scales. Any score above the 75th percentile indicates an interest in that area. Very low scores indicate that a person is not interested in that area. The inventory takes approximately 40 minutes to complete.

Ohio Vocational Interest Survey (OVIS II): Grades 7–12, College, Adult. This survey combines an interest inventory with an optional Career Planning Questionnaire. The inventory consists of 253 job activities that students respond to on a five-point scale from "Like very much" to "Dislike very much." On the printout of results (one edition is hand-scorable), students see how they ranked 23 major occupational areas, whether their interest for each area falls into the low, average, or high interest range, and how their interests compare with other students nationally. The Career Planner is a 16-page workbook designed to help students explore career possibilities in light of their OVIS II results. The inventory takes about 50 minutes; the Career Planner booklet an additional 30. A microcomputer version is also available.

Self-Directed Search: Grades 9–12, College, Adult. This self-paced inventory is popular with high school guidance departments. Students respond to questions concerning their aspirations, activities, competencies, self-estimates of abilities, and their occupational goals. After recording their answers in the Assessment Booklet, students turn to the Occupations Finder, which lists a wide range of occupational possibilities, divided into categories based on personality types: Realistic, Investigative, Artistic, Social, Enterprising, and Conventional. A special form, Form E, is written at the fourth-grade level and the self-scoring system is simplified. The Self-Directed Search takes about 40 minutes.

Strong-Campbell Interest Inventory (SCII): Grades 11–12, College, Adults. Many schools find the Strong-Campbell too expensive to administer to groups of students. It has to be computer-scored and the report information is extensive. Nevertheless, it is commonly available, especially through private counseling services. The inventory compares a person's interests with those of people successfully employed in a wide variety of occupations. There are 6 General Occupational Themes (the same as those that appear on the Self-Directed Search); 23 Basic Interest Scales that measure strength and consistency of interest in specific areas; 207 Occupational Scales that indicate how similar a person's interests are to those of individuals in particular occupations; and Special Scales—Academic Comfort and Introversion-Extroversion—that are useful in professional counseling. The inventory takes approximately 30 to 40 minutes.

Wide-Range Interest-Opinion Test: Age 5 through Adult. This test uses pictures for measuring a person's interests and attitudes related to career planning or work involvement. It can be administered to groups with responses self-recorded, or individually administered to persons whose age, mental ability, or physical limitations restrict their ability to complete the answer document. The test consists of 150 sets of 3 pictures each: the person looks at the picture and records whether the activity is liked or disliked. The test is untimed and takes about 40 minutes.

Other career interest and decision-making surveys include:

Career Decision-Making System: Grade 6 and above

Career Decision Scale: Grades 9–12, College

Career Guidance Inventory in Trades, Services and Technologies: Grade 9 and above

Career Maturity Inventory: Grades 6–12, College, Adult

Jackson Vocational Interest Survey: Grade 7 through Adult

JOB-O and Career Exploration Series: Grade 7 and above

Minnesota Importance Questionnaire: Grade 9 and above

Myers Briggs Type Indicator: Grade 7 and above

Occ-U-Sort: Grade 7 and above

Planning Career Goals: Grades 8–12

Reading Free Vocational Interest Inventory: Ages 13 through Adult, Mentally Retarded or Learning Disabled

Social and Prevocational Information Battery: Grades 6–12 and above, Mildly Retarded

Exploring Your Child's Aptitudes

Discovering your child's interests is just the first step; measuring his or her *aptitudes* is next.

Aptitude is the ease with which a person can learn to do something. Ever since the movie *Top Gun* was released, for example, I've had a number of students talk to me about their desire to fly for the Air Force. My first question is, "Do you like math?" To those who don't, I explain that mathematics is the key to flying and that pilots have a higher-than-average aptitude for math. I also tell them about the range of courses they'll have to do well in to qualify for flight training. I then go on to describe other opportunities in the Air Force that don't require an aptitude for math.

The following tests measure aptitude and the results are helpful in making career plans.

The Armed Services Vocational Aptitude Battery (ASVAB): Grade 10 through Adult. The ASVAB is a free, two-and-a-half hour aptitude test, usually given to juniors and seniors and to all new military recruits. High school guidance departments can administer it to groups or a student can call the local recruiter and set a test date. There's no military obligation.

The test measures the following general *abilities* (already learned skills): numerical operations, attention to detail, word knowledge, electronic information, arithmetic reasoning, space perception, mathematics knowledge, mechanical comprehension, general science, shop information, automotive information, and general information. The scores from these "mini-tests" are combined into aptitude averages: verbal, mathematical, perceptual speed, mechanical, health/social/technology, and academic.

Students and their counselors both receive a copy of the scores. Students who are thinking about majoring in business at college, for instance, would probably like to know how they did on the mathematical or academic ability portions of the test. Military recruiters also receive a copy of the scores. They can advise students about which jobs they would qualify for in the armed services based on their test results. For a job as an aircraft mechanic, for example, the Army might require a score of at least a 45 in the mechanical area. To be a computer operator, the Air Force might require a 40 in the health, social and technology area. Students who are qualified in more than one area can choose from a number of jobs.

If your child wants to prepare for the ASVAB, he or she can check out from the school library, or purchase at a local bookstore, a copy of *Practice for Army Placement Tests* (Arco Publishing 1982). This book explains the ASVAB and has pages of sample questions covering all parts of the test.

Differential Aptitude Tests: Grades 8–12. This battery of eight aptitude tests in verbal reasoning, numerical ability, abstract reasoning, clerical speed and accuracy, mechanical reasoning, space relations, spelling, and language usage is designed for educational and vocational use in junior and senior high schools. The battery yields nine scores including an index of scholastic ability; consequently, it's also an intelligence test and counselors are encouraged to use it for that purpose.

The Career Planning Program can be administered with the basic test: students record their educational and vocational plans and preferences on a questionnaire. This information is combined with the student's scores on the eight individual aptitude tests to produce a Career Planning Report. The report either confirms the appropriateness of the student's occupational choices in light of his or her abilities and interests, or suggests alternative occupational areas to explore. The combined tests take slightly over three hours. A software version is also available.

How to Use the Results of Interest Surveys and Aptitude Tests

Surveys and tests of any sort are potentially intimidating. After all, the person answering the questions knows that whoever wrote the test is trying to "get at something" and the results are, in a sense, a pronouncement. Your child, having been tested in school, having tried out for teams and plays, will attempt to read either praise or criticism into the results of a career interest survey or aptitude test. "It says I'm not good at anything, right?" "Well, I guess I ought to think about going into social work if that's what it says." Try to help your son or daughter see that the results are neither a judgment nor a directive. Instead, point out that, first, a test or a survey only gathers information from a person on *that particular day and during that particular time.* Results can be influenced by a kid in the room with a cold whose constant nose-blowing distracts everyone. Second, the results are an *indication,* not a verdict. In other words, they are intended to be used as advice, not as means to reveal a person's destiny. In fact, the value of any test or survey increases when results are discussed with a professional. So I recommend that once your child has some scores to work with, the two of you make an appointment to see a resource person at your school or in the community.

Questions to Ask Your Child's Counselor

Times being what they are in the guidance area of education, your child's counselor may have a big counselee load—lots of young people to schedule into classes and perhaps even supervise in the lunchroom.

Nevertheless, he or she can help interpret any survey or test administered by the school, plus direct you to other resources in the school. You can help make your appointment especially worthwhile by doing a bit of preparation beforehand.

First, when you make the appointment, request a reasonable amount of time—say, half an hour—so that the counselor can schedule you accordingly.

Second, be specific about what you'd like to discuss: your child's results on the Ohio Vocational Interest Survey, for example. Or you can say that you're coming in for some advice about career planning. This way, the counselor can assemble a few things you might want to look at, or pull out your child's file ahead of time and give some thought to the kind of advice you're seeking.

Third, get an unofficial copy of your child's transcript—the record of grades and courses taken—from the school registrar so that you can see the academic direction your son or daughter seems to be taking. The more realistic understanding you have of your child's abilities or performance, the less likely you'll come to the appointment with misconceptions.

Finally, realize that the counselor is *your child's advocate*; it's not his or her job to bring your child around to your point of view, necessarily. Occasionally, parents will come to see me with the notion that I'm supposed to make their child see that mom or dad is right. Sometimes, of course, they are right, but counselors are not just hired guns. They are information-givers, experts on how the school works, professionals whose highest ethical priority is to help make clear what's in a child's best interests.

Here are some questions you can ask that will tap exactly what a counselor can offer:

- Is my child in a college prep or a vocational program of study?
- What percentage of students at this school go on to college?
- What is the guidance department's program for helping students make career and college decisions as they move through high school?
- How often will my child see you? Must an appointment be made or is counseling regularly scheduled?
- Would you please tell me your interpretation of my child's interest survey or aptitude test results?
- How will the results of the survey or aptitude test be used?
- Based on the results of the interest survey or aptitude test my child took, is she taking courses that parallel her interests?

- Does the school have any special opportunities—a gifted program or cooperative education, for example—that we should look into?
- Can you refer us to any services in the community that could help us with our post-high-school plans?

If your child is receiving special services at the school, or if you have questions about what's available in this area, make an appointment to see the school's social worker or school psychologist. Follow the same pre-appointment steps described above for meeting with the counselor.

Questions to Ask a School Psychologist or Social Worker

- What do my son's or daughter's overall ability and academic skill levels suggest in terms of appropriate alternatives or challenges? (four-year university, two-year community college, trade or technical school, entry-level employment, vocational training program with close supervision, etc.)
- What are the implications of my son's or daughter's learning disability (emotional problem, mental impairment)?
- What are the implications of my child's learning style? (In other words, are there aspects of his or her learning profile that should guide our decision making?)
- How can I identify my child's career interests?
- What testing is available in or out of school that can help me determine whether my child has the requisite skills for his or her post-high-school plans?
- How can I motivate my son or daughter?
- What referral sources for counseling are there for my child's learning disability, hearing or visual impairment, emotional problem, etc.
- What associations might I contact to get further information about my child's difficulties?
- What resources within the school might be used prior to graduation to help my child explore post-high-school alternatives?
- Are there things you can suggest that we might do to enhance my

child's learning and/or personal development? (For example, compensatory strategies, remedial activities, or the use of tools such as a tape recorder, word processor, calculator, etc.)

Using a Private Counselor

Some parents turn to private counselors because they want their children to receive more help with career or college plans than perhaps the school has time to give. In this case, it's important to find the right kind of professional.

Independent college counselors will help your child choose a college, fill out an application, write an application essay if one is required, and sometimes go to bat for your child with a college admission office. Independent college counselors don't often help with career planning, however.

Private vocational and psychological services are often a group of practitioners who offer individual counseling, vocational testing and interpretation, and in some cases, job-hunting help.

Individual practitioners may be psychologists who specialize in adolescent counseling. They might refer you to colleagues who can help with areas of special concern to you and your child.

Before you make a commitment, however, follow these steps:

Ask for a description of the types of services that will be provided.

Ask about the fee: is it a flat figure, or assessed per visit, or based on a sliding scale?

Ask whether you will be required to sign a contract. What are the terms?

Ask for a reference you can call.

By asking these questions in advance, you'll avoid potential misunderstandings.

Finally, there are community and state resources available to you, as well. Look in the Yellow Pages of your telephone directory under "Social Service Organizations," "Psychiatric Social Workers," "Psychologists," or in the White Pages under the name of your state. Also, refer to the Appendix in this book for the addresses and phone numbers of state or regional career information centers. Ask for recommendations on resources in your area.

A Career Interest Survey *You* Can Administer

Exploring your child's interests takes work. As I said at the beginning of Chapter 3, your child is complex. Don't be discouraged by that complexity; try to view your child as a fascinating collection of talents, interests, and partially formed plans for the future. The more concrete information about career possibilities you gather as a result of interest surveys and advice from professionals, the better you'll understand where your youngster is headed.

As a first step, give the Shields's Career Interest Inventory to your son or daughter. Find a quiet place where the work can be done in one sitting, then review the results together. This inventory has been adapted from the Career Interest Inventory developed by the student services staff of Prairie State College in Chicago Heights, Illinois, and administered to all incoming freshmen. You may want to take it yourself—it's fun!

Shields's Career Interest Inventory

Dear Student:

As part of this book on helping young people find the right careers, I've included an *interest inventory* for you. It's *not a test* and it won't tell you what you should do with your life, but it can help you:

- identify some things about yourself that are related to being successful at certain kinds of work;
- investigate some career alternatives you may not have thought of yet;
- target some potentially satisfying jobs.

A survey of this type has nothing to do with intelligence: all that counts is honest answers about what you like and dislike when it comes to doing different types of work. Also, there are some places where you have to describe yourself a little: this too will depend on straightforward answers that only you can give.

You can use a pen or pencil—you'll score it at the end yourself. (Enter scores on page 50.) If you can, try to do the whole survey at one sitting.

PRACTICAL TYPE

Yes	No	
☐	☐	I think I am practical and conventional.
☐	☐	I sometimes have trouble expressing myself in words.
☐	☐	I like working with objects more than ideas.
☐	☐	I have popular political opinions.
☐	☐	I think about new ideas or fads for a while before I try them.
☐	☐	I usually can mend or repair things.
☐	☐	I have ability for outdoor work.
☐	☐	I use hand tools or machines skillfully.
☐	☐	I can work where there is risk, danger, or adventure.
☐	☐	I can perform activities that require physical coordination.
☐	☐	I am interested in agriculture.
☐	☐	I am interested in nature and/or adventure activities.
☐	☐	I am interested in military activities.
☐	☐	I am interested in mechanical activities.

Total **Yes** answers _____ (Practical Score). Enter on scoring page.

Characteristics of practical people: circle the traits that apply to you.

Agreeable	Money-minded	Bashful
Candid	Informal	Normal
Honest	Persevering	Frugal
Quiet	Realistic	

Sample careers for practical people: circle ones that interest you.

Air conditioning technician	Fire fighter	Painter
Air traffic controller	Forester	Plumber
Architectural technician	Heavy equipment	Police officer
Bus driver	operator	Tool and die maker
Dressmaker	Jeweler	Welder
Emergency medical	Machinist	
technician	Nursery worker	

Practical people leisure activities: circle ones that interest you.

Archery	Flying	Mountain climbing
Auto repair	Fly tying	Pet training
Athletics	Gardening	Skin diving
Motorcycling	Hiking	Water skiing
Farming	Machine shop work	Wood working
Fishing	Metal scupture	Whittling

Total number of items circled from lists above _____. Enter on scoring page.

People with high Practical scores and interests are strong, aggressive, and physically skillful. They usually prefer working with objects and things more than with people or ideas. They may have difficulty putting their feelings into words.

INTELLECTUAL TYPE

Yes	No	
☐	☐	I usually think through a problem before acting on it.
☐	☐	I like working alone more than with a group of people.
☐	☐	I like to see how things work by taking them apart and asking questions.
☐	☐	I like to stay away from situations that have many rules to follow.
☐	☐	I like to find my own solution to problems.
☐	☐	I like to learn about myself and the world around me.
☐	☐	I search through many possibilities for a solution.
☐	☐	I try to create ways of doing a job.
☐	☐	I get so involved in an activity that I lose track of time.
☐	☐	I can solve complex problems.
☐	☐	I am interested in science.
☐	☐	I am interested in mathematics.
☐	☐	I am interested in medical science.
☐	☐	I am interested in research.

Total **Yes** answers _____ (Intellectual Score). Enter on scoring page.

Characteristics of intellectual people: circle the traits that apply to you.

Logical	Self-sufficient	Humble
Careful	Thoughtful	Exact
Judgmental	Introspective	Sensible
Investigative	Experimental	Reticent

Sample careers for intellectual people: circle ones that interest you.

Airplane pilot	Economist	Physician
Astronomer	Electronic systems	Production planner
Biologist	tester	Quality control technician
Chemist	Electronics technician	Radiological technician
Computer operator	Engineer	Research analyst
Data programmer	Geologist	Respiratory therapist
Dentist	Medical lab technician	X-ray technician

Intellectual people leisure activities: circle ones that interest you.

Artifact collecting	Chess playing	Model making
Abstract art	Folklore	Nature hikes
Anthropology	Fossil collecting	Philosophy
Astrology	History	Reading
Bird watching	Laboratory	Travel
Butterfly collecting	experimenting	
Cave exploration	Mineral collecting	

Total number of items circled from lists above _____. Enter on scoring page.

Individuals with high Intellectual scores and interests are original, creative, and task oriented. They usually enjoy solving abstract problems and working to understand the physical world. They often have unconventional values and attitudes and prefer unstructured settings with freedom to think problems through.

CREATIVE TYPE

Yes   No

☐   ☐   I prefer to make my own plans for a project than to be given plans.

☐   ☐   I like to create things that are different.

☐   ☐   I like to be independent.

☐   ☐   I prefer to express myself in writing or through art rather than through speaking.

☐   ☐   I like privacy when I am creating.

☐   ☐   I can create the new, the unusual.

☐   ☐   I can express myself through drama, art, music, or writing.

☐   ☐   I can design clothes, furniture, ceramics, or posters.

☐   ☐   I can write creatively.

☐   ☐   I have ability in music or drama.

☐   ☐   I am interested in music.

☐   ☐   I am interested in dramatics.

☐   ☐   I am interested in art.

☐   ☐   I am interested in writing.

Total **Yes** answers _____ (Creative Score). Enter on the scoring page.

Characteristics of creative people: circle the traits that apply to you.

Complex	Spontaneous	Independent
Disorganized	Imaginative	Artistic
Demonstrative	Impractical	Nonconforming
Impressionable	Impetuous	Visionary

Sample careers for creative people: circle ones that interest you.

Actor/actress	Drama teacher	Literature teacher
Advertising executive	Fashion illustrator	Music teacher/
Apparel designer	Foreign language	musician
Architect	interpreter	Photographer
Architectural technician	Interior designer	Public relations person
Art teacher	Journalist/reporter	Writer

Creative people leisure activities: circle the ones that interest you.

Basketry	Decorating	Painting
Cartooning	Dramatics	Percussion
Carving	Flower arranging	Piano
Ceramics	Flower growing	Poetry
Crafts	Guitar playing	Sculpture
Creative writing	Music composing	Singing

Total number of items circled _____. Enter total on scoring page.

Individuals with high Artistic scores and interests are often sensitive, emotional, unconventional in outlook, and have a great need for self-expression. They may be reluctant to assert their opinions or capabilities except through their art. This type of person scores higher on originality than any other type.

OUTGOING TYPE

Yes	No	
☐	☐	I think most people are easy to get along with.
☐	☐	I usually feel good about expressing myself verbally.
☐	☐	I prefer solving a problem by discussing it rather than by analyzing it on paper.
☐	☐	I think I am a very responsible person.
☐	☐	I like being asked to take a leadership role.
☐	☐	I can easily meet people and make new friends.
☐	☐	I can plan and host parties or entertain people well.
☐	☐	I am skillful in helping people who have problems.
☐	☐	I can lead a charity or benefit drive.
☐	☐	I am skillful in leading a discussion.
☐	☐	I am interested in social science.
☐	☐	I am interested in teaching.
☐	☐	I am interested in medical service.
☐	☐	I am interested in religious activities.

Total **Yes** answers _____ (Social Score). Enter total on scoring page.

Characteristics of outgoing people: circle the traits that apply to you.

Sincere	Unreserved	Sympathetic
A joiner	Considerate	Tactful
Hospitable	A peacemaker	Sociable
Generous	Warmhearted	Understanding

Sample careers for outgoing people: circle the careers that interest you.

Athletic coach	Hair stylist	Physical therapist
Child care worker	Home economist	Politician
Cosmetologist	Interviewer	Recreation director
Counselor	Librarian	Social worker
Dental assistant	Minister	Teacher
Dietician	Nurse	Training director
Food service manager	Parole officer	

Outgoing people leisure activities: circle ones that interest you.

Bridge	Golf	Spectator sports
Church activities	Interest clubs	Square dancing
Civic activities	Opera	Theater
Dancing	Politics	Travel
Dominoes	Quartet singing	Volunteer service
Fraternal clubs	Scouting	

Total number of items circled _____. Enter total on scoring page.

Individuals with a high Social score and interests are usually sociable, responsible, humanistic, and caring people. They tend to express themselves well and prefer to solve problems through discussion or by working with people on an interpersonal level. They often like to be the center of attention or be near the center of activity.

PERSUASIVE TYPE

Yes	No	
☐	☐	I enjoy talking more than listening when in a group of people.
☐	☐	I have no problem explaining my ideas.
☐	☐	I like being in charge of activities.
☐	☐	I often find myself trying to change someone's point of view.
☐	☐	I am always ready to try something that hasn't been done before.
☐	☐	I can sell things.
☐	☐	I can operate my own business.
☐	☐	I can manage a business for someone else.
☐	☐	I can influence others to my point of view.
☐	☐	I can compete with others in my work.
☐	☐	I am interested in public speaking.
☐	☐	I am interested in law and/or sales.
☐	☐	I am interested in merchandising and/or sales.
☐	☐	I am interested in business management.

Total **Yes** answers _____ (Persuasive Score). Enter total on scoring page.

Characteristics of persuasive people: circle the traits that apply to you.

Adventurous	Active	Self-confident
A go-getter	Spontaneous	Sociable
Attention-getting	Enthusiastic	Popular
Commanding	Fun-loving	

Sample careers for persuasive people: circle the ones that interest you.

Attorney	Personnel manager	Sales manager
Banker	Purchasing agent	Salesperson
Business manager	Radio/TV announcer	Systems analyst
Contractor	Real estate	Traffic manager
Industrial engineer	salesperson	Warehouse manager
Labor arbitrator	Retail merchant	

Persuasive people leisure activities: circle ones that interest you.

After dinner speaking	Hostessing	Pottery
Antique collecting	Income tax service	Raising plants
Book writing	Jewelry making	Saddlery
Furniture making	Landscaping	Selling
Gun collecting	Leathercraft	Shoeing horses
Horse breeding	Photography	Taxidermy

Total number of items circled _____. Enter total on scoring page.

Individuals with high Persuasive scores and interests are usually energetic, enthusiastic, self-confident, and enjoy persuading others to their viewpoints. They often prefer power, status, and material wealth to precise, long-term intellectual effort.

ADAPTIVE TYPE

Yes	No	
☐	☐	I like to know exactly what is expected of me in a new situation.
☐	☐	I would like to be part of a large well-established organization.
☐	☐	I would rather be given directions than to figure them out for myself.
☐	☐	I need to understand things that are going on around me.
☐	☐	I can usually keep my cool and not lose my temper in times of stress.
☐	☐	I can do office work well.
☐	☐	I can keep records of my own expenses.
☐	☐	I can organize and set up files.
☐	☐	I can work in a routine work setting.
☐	☐	I can use office machines.
☐	☐	I am interested in office practices.
☐	☐	I am interested in accounting.
☐	☐	I am interested in finance.
☐	☐	I am interested in business education.

Total **Yes** answers _____ (Adaptive Score). Enter total on scoring page.

Characteristics of adaptive people: circle traits that apply to you.

Conventional	Reasonable	Reliable
Responsible	Organized	Calm
Careful	Productive	Compliant
Obliging	Practical	

Sample careers for adaptive people: circle ones that interest you.

Accountant	Clerk stenographer	Office machine operator
Biller	Credit manager	Receptionist
Bookkeeper	File clerk	Secretary
Business teacher	Finance expert	Time study analyst
Certified public accountant	Key punch operator	Typist

Adaptive people leisure activities: circle ones that interest you.

Autograph collecting	Embroidering	Post card collecting
Book collecting	Enameling	Sewing
China collecting	Knitting	Stamp collecting
Cooking	Lace making	Weaving
Crocheting	Lamp collecting	
Diary writing	Leather working	

Total number of items circled _____. Enter total on scoring page.

Individuals with high Adaptive scores and interests prefer highly structured verbal and numerical activities. They seem to work best in well-established chains of command. They tend to value material possessions and status more than physical skills or personal relationships.

SUMMARY OF SCORES

Enter your scores from the previous pages.

	Yes Scores		Circled Items		Total Score
Occupational Types					
Practical Score	_____	+	_____	=	_____
Intellectual Score	_____	+	_____	=	_____
Creative Score	_____	+	_____	=	_____
Outgoing Score	_____	+	_____	=	_____
Persuasive Score	_____	+	_____	=	_____
Adaptive Score	_____	+	_____	=	_____

Write in the names of your three highest occupational types.

Highest score category _____ Type

Second highest score _____ Type

Third highest score _____ Type

Now go back and review the sample careers in each of your three highest areas. List any careers from these areas which still seem interesting to you.

Career Possibilities

_____	_____
_____	_____
_____	_____

Finally, look over the college degree programs (two- and four-year) listed below, grouped according to occupational types. Put a check in the boxes of your three highest categories. Circle any of the academic programs in these categories which seem interesting to you.

☐ *Practical programs*

Engineering	Architectural drafting	Metallurgy
Forestry	Agronomy	Fire science
Physical education	Robotics	Hydraulics
Police science	Construction technologies	Automotive services

☐ *Intellectual programs*

Biological sciences	Medicine	Engineering
Chemistry	Pharmacy	Mathematics
Computer science	Psychology	Electronics
Dentistry	Veterinary medicine	technology
Medical	Geology	Data processing
technology	Economics	

☐ *Creative programs*

Architecture	Journalism	Interior design
Art	Literature	Photography
Broadcasting	Music	Fashion illustration
English	Theater	Public relations
Foreign languages	Graphic design	Advertising

☐ *Outgoing programs*

Anthropology	Child development	Physical therapy
Education	Dental hygiene	Social work
Political science	Nursing	Physical education
Speech	Teacher assisting	Cosmetology

☐ *Persuasive programs*

Banking	Finance	Insurance
Management	Sports administration	Labor relations
Marketing	Hotel/motel management	Human resources
Real estate	Law	Public administration

☐ *Adaptive programs*

Accounting	Medical secretarial science	Office management
Bookkeeping	Legal secretarial science	
Credit	Court reporting	
management	Taxation	

In which three categories did you circle the most programs?

_____

_____

_____

Are these the same as the three occupational types you scored in?

5

How Labor Market
Trends Will Affect
Your Child

"Good morning! It's a balmy 71 degrees at 5:45 a.m. in the city of Albu-
querque on this Thursday, May 7, 1998." Your daughter reaches up, turns
off the radio, and sits up in bed. Time to go to work. Her husband has
already left, in time for his early flight. She thinks about what she'll need to
take with her today: a new box of disposable diapers (she can go down to the
office daycare center during lunch—but wait—she's having a "working
lunch" with two new clients to go over their investments—she'd better drop
the diapers off first thing); and she'd better remember to bring her exercise
outfit so she can work out in the company gym before checking out at 5:30.
"Well," she thinks as she stretches, "time to get a move on."

This scenario is not too different from the way many young women
live today, is it? You'll notice she's living in the Southwest—over 60
percent of the population will live in the South and West by the mid-
1990s—and that her work environment is adapted to the needs of
parents. Also, she's involved in an area of finance, which will be one
of the fastest-growing industrial sectors over the next decade. Other
than that, she's a working mom (women will account for three-fifths
of the growth in the labor force by then) and like many of us, she
works from nine to five.

In fact, labor forecasts about the working world through the 1990s
paint a picture of a worklife that is not radically different from the one

53

most of us know now. Computers, flex-time, robots, and advances in telecommunications will increase the efficiency of workers, but scenarios of us flying to work from high rises above the earth are still a long way off. However, some developments do hold important implications for your child's future.

Being born in the generation after the Baby Boomers will continue to be like being behind a truck on a two-lane road: competition for jobs with status and high income will be tough because there will be so many workers in their prime years. Technology will increase the amount of goods and services each worker can produce, causing some dislocation of other workers. The educational level of the workforce overall will continue to rise. How will these trends affect your child?

Demographics Means Jobs

Population growth in the United States has been rising and falling unevenly over the past 50 years, creating troughs and crests in the age structure of the overall population. People who are approaching retirement today were born around the time of the Depression. There weren't many of them, so they didn't have to cope with an oversupply of workers their own age. The Baby Boomers who followed broke all records in sheer number, causing school boards to hold classes in churches and national magazines to feature pictures of legions of young mothers with strollers. By the time Baby Boomers were college age, it had become clear that there would be an overabundance of young workers competing for jobs. Many Boomers who graduated from college were forced to take jobs that didn't require a college education.

The birth rate dropped drastically in the 1970s and early 1980s resulting in another trough. So at present the picture looks like this: an enormous segment of the population, the Baby Boomers, are trying to squeeze into jobs being left vacant by exiting Depression-era children. And coming behind the Boomers is a smaller group that will find, when they go job-hunting, the jobs they want are being held on to by people born during the two-and-a-half decades after World War II.

What does this mean for your child? Probably that there will be plenty of entry-level jobs for young people; first, because there are fewer young workers, and second, because today's lifestyle requires all kinds of time-saving services—such as fast-food establishments that offer waitressing, burger flipping, and maintenance types of jobs. But it will be hard for the younger generation to move out of low-level jobs (in white-collar fields, too) because openings further up the ladder will be scarce. Once the Baby Boomers begin to retire, there will finally be an upsurge in the number of available high-income positions.

However, a kind of wild card that operates in labor market predictions is technology, and we need to consider that influence next.

Technology Is a Catalyst

Seventy-five years ago there were 11 million people working on American farms, producing 100 percent of our national food supply. Today, there are fewer than 3 million people on farms, but they produce 125 percent of our food supply. The reason? Technology has boosted the output per worker tremendously, reducing the number of workers needed.

Technology has had a similar impact on other types of work. A well-known example is the use of robots in automobile assembly plants. General Motors plans to have 14,000 robots in place by 1990, displacing 40,000 to 50,000 of its workers. If these workers are willing to be retrained, they won't be out of a job. But how many *new* jobs will actually be created versus how many will be lost to improved efficiency is hard to predict. And that's why technology is a wild card. If labor forecasters only had to estimate how many workers will have to be replaced over the years due to death, job-changing, or retirement, then the number of openings in occupations would be simple to arrive at. But whether technology will create enough previously unheard of jobs—robot trainers, repairers, and technicians in the auto industry, for example—or whether industry-by-industry totals will show an overall decline in the number of available jobs, it's hard to say.

Educational Levels of Workers Will Increase

More people are getting more education today than in previous generations. A century ago, one person in 100 graduated from high school; today, 86 out of 100 graduate. A century ago, one person in 100 graduated from college; today, 21 out of 100 graduate. Between 1970 and 1984, the percentage of the labor force with at least one year of college increased from 26 to 41 percent; with four or more years of college from 13 to 22 percent. This trend will continue, and job-seekers of the next decade should be aware that employers will have higher expectations about applicants' educational levels. Their expectations will be founded on the belief that "smarter" employees will be better employees, so naturally they will continue to look for workers with the best credentials. The best response your child can prepare in the face of this development is to go on in school as far as he or she can.

Some parents and children wonder what kind of education will be the best bulwark against change—a degree in business, a certificate in electronics, a law degree? But new ideas are constantly changing the ways we live and work, so the real answer is that *no particular kind of education is the best.* Instead, it would be a good idea for you to foster in your child the desire to continue education throughout life. In other words, encourage your child to concentrate on a field that appeals to her or him, but recognize that lifelong learning will become one of the keys to success. The Spanish major who lands a job in a bank, and enjoys it, will have to take a few night courses—certainly some bank-sponsored seminars—to stay viable, promotable. The young man who rises to manager of a recreation facility will have to supplement his education with classes in personnel management or exercise physiology—whatever is needed to stay on the cutting edge.

You can lay the groundwork for a lifetime of learning by closely monitoring your child's progress in school and making sure that he or she is proficient in the fundamentals—reading, writing, self-expression, history, research, computation—so that later these tools can be applied to unlock doors of opportunity through continued education. Another suggestion is that you set the example yourself and enroll in some enrichment classes, then share your satisfaction at learning new skills, such as how to service your car, how to buy stocks, or how to appreciate symphonic music. Make it clear education is like exercise: one of its main purposes is to enhance our capacity to meet the challenges of living.

Now let's see what the future seems to hold for all industries and general types of occupations. We'll categorize them as having a *good employment outlook, average employment outlook,* and *poor employment outlook.*

The Big Picture: Industries

Industries are divided into two broad groups: *goods-producing industries,* which produce tangibles such as refrigerators, coal, and cars; and *service-producing industries,* which produce intangibles such as insurance, education, health care, and entertainment. Within the two broad categories, labor experts subdivide occupations into nine industrial sectors. Under service-producing industries they are transportation, communication, and public utilities; trade; finance, insurance, and real estate; services; and government. Goods-producing industries are subdivided into agriculture; mining; construction; and manufacturing.

Today, most jobs (7 out of 10) are in the service-producing industries. As people's incomes and standard of living have increased over the years, they have added services to their lives more rapidly than goods. Also, many goods-producing industries themselves utilize service industries in the course of doing business. Service industries will continue to be the leaders in growth, providing more jobs than goods-producing industries. Between now and 1995, 9 out of 10 new jobs will be in service industries.

Good Employment Outlook

Trade. As the population has grown and incomes have risen, people have been able to afford more goods and services. Wholesale and retail trade has benefited from this. Eating and drinking places in particular will continue to offer the greatest number of jobs in the coming decade within the trade sector.

Services. Between now and 1995, this sector will offer more new jobs than any of the other eight industrial sectors. Services is a catch-all category for a variety of industries such as travel agencies, hotels, consulting firms, and beauty shops. Like jobs in the trade sector, salaries for these occupations range from very low to high, depending on the position.

Finance, Insurance, Real Estate. New kinds of financial instruments—IRAs, zero-coupon bonds and others—combined with new types of financial services such as financial planning and investment counseling made this industrial sector one of the fastest growing in the 1980s. This will continue to be true, except that automation and computer-aided services will limit the number of new jobs since fewer people will be needed to do more work.

Average Employment Outlook

Transportation, communication, and public utilities. Some types of transportation—trucking and local transit—will experience significant growth, while others—air, water, and railroad transportation—will make an average to less-than-average showing. Likewise, communications will maintain an average rate of growth, except for businesses that benefit from telephone deregulation; these will offer many new jobs. New construction will require public utilities, providing a dependable but not generous number of new jobs in this area.

Manufacturing. Manufacturing was affected by two almost simultaneous developments in the late 1970s that continued into the 1980s: improved productivity through technology, which decreased the number of new jobs, and competition from foreign manufacturers, which led to additional lay-offs. Although the manufacturing sector is not expected to reach its previous employment peaks, certain types of manufacturing, such as scientific instruments, computers, and materials handling equipment, will offer more jobs than other areas.

Construction. Construction is sensitive to changes in the investment outlook; new building and housing starts depend on capital and interest. Indications are, however, that construction-related jobs will be available in steady but modest numbers over the next decade.

Government. Goals set by the Reagan administration curtailed the growth of federal jobs, but state and local governments will continue to offer new jobs at an average rate.

Poor Employment Outlook

Agriculture. Although international demand for food will increase in the next decade, improved methods of farming will meet the challenge without increasing the number of U.S. farmers or farm workers. Only agribusiness, which includes farm management, soil sampling, and crop analysis, for example, holds out the promise of new jobs in a sector that is otherwise destined to have declining numbers of workers.

Mining. There was a brief surge in the number of mining-related new jobs when oil became temporarily expensive and a search was launched to find new domestic pockets of oil and gas. But world surpluses have since depressed the price of these resources, and mining jobs will probably continue to dwindle.

Scaled-Down Pictures: Occupational Clusters

Slicing the job outlook even finer uncovers occuptional clusters. Clusters are groups of jobs that require similar aptitudes, interests, education, and training. At this point, because individual jobs may vary in outlook within the cluster, it's best to organize them all by some yardstick. Below is a chart of the 75 occupations with the most promising outlook through 1995, cluster by cluster. For more information about individual occupations, see the *Occupational Outlook Handbook*, published by the U.S. Department of Labor. It's available in most school and public libraries.

Cluster	Occupation	Outlook/Advice
Executive, Administrative, and Managerial Occupations	Accountants and auditors	Managers will rely more on accounting information to make decisions.
	Bank officers and managers	Banks will expand services.
	Construction supervisors	Increased standards for safe construction will create more jobs of this type.
	Health services administrators	Demand for health services will increase and health services will become more complex.
	Hotel managers and assistants	Best opportunities will be for persons with degree in hotel management.
	Medical records administrators	Insurance companies and governmental agencies will require more complete medical information as size of elderly population increases.
Engineers, Surveyors, and Architects	Architects	Employment expected to rise faster than average.
	Landscape architects	New construction and city and regional environment planning will lead to new jobs.

Cluster	Occupation	Outlook/Advice
Engineers, Surveyors, and Architects (continued)	Engineers	Employment expected to grow faster than average.
	Aerospace engineers	Employment will rise faster than average in response to increased expenditures for military and commercial aircraft.
	Agricultural engineers	Worldwide demand for food will spur interest in improving food production through technological means.
	Biomedical engineers	Advances in treatment of disease and organ transplants will generate additional research and design.
	Ceramic engineers	Recent breakthroughs in superconductivity make this one of the hottest research fields.
	Civil engineers	New construction coupled with environmental concerns will offer many new jobs.
	Electrical/ electronics engineers	Faster-than-average growth due to demand for increased consumer goods.
	Industrial engineers	Expansion of automated processes and increased interest in improved efficiency and safety will provide new jobs.
	Mechanical engineers	Reasons for growth are similar to those above.
	Metallurgical engineers	Recycling, new alloys, and general research will lead to new jobs.
Natural Scientists and Mathematicians	Systems analysts	Increased computer capabilities and increased usage of computers will require more analysts.
	Geologists	Domestic mineral exploration will increase.

Cluster	Occupation	Outlook/Advice
Social Scientists, Social Workers, Religious Workers, and Lawyers	Lawyers	Demand for increasingly specialized legal services will increase.
	Economists	Employment expected to grow faster than average.
	Market research analysts	Demand for new products will stimulate marketing activities.
	Urban and regional planners	Increasing demand for environmental, economic, and energy planning.
Teachers, Librarians, and Counselors	Elementary teachers	A "boomlet" created by percent of Baby Boomers having children will create major need for elementary teachers.
Health Diagnosing and Treating Practitioners	Optometrists	Aging of the population will lead to increased need for eye care.
	Physicians	Creative new health care delivery systems will provide opportunities for physicians.
	Podiatrists	Interest in fitness will mean more jobs for podiatrists.
Registered Nurses, Pharmacists, Dieticians, Therapists, and Physician Assistants	Dieticians	Demand for proper nutrition and food management will mean new jobs.
	Occupational therapists	Occupational therapy programs will multiply.
	Pharmacists	An aging population will increase the use of pharmacists in health care institutions.
	Physical therapists	The public's concern for rehabilitation services will grow.
	Registered nurses	Experts predict a critical shortage of nurses.
	Respiratory therapy workers	New applications of respiratory therapy will be used in treating diseases.

Cluster	Occupation	Outlook/Advice
Registered Nurses, Pharmacists, Dieticians, Therapists, and Physician Assistants (continued)	Speech pathologists and audiologists	Public concern over speech and hearing disorders will increase as the population ages.
	Dental hygienists	Growing awareness of importance of dental care will increase the demand for dental hygienists.
	Licensed practical nurses	Aging population will demand more health care.
	Medical laboratory workers	Experts predict increased use of medical laboratory tests in the diagnosis and treatment of disease.
	Medical records technicians and clerks	Increased paperwork in hospitals and health care facilities will require more records technicians and clerks.
	Radiologic (X-ray) technologists	New uses will be found for use of X-ray equipment in the diagnosis and treatment of disease.
	Surgical technicians	Number of operations will increase; technicians will assume nurses' role in operating room.
Writers, Artists, and Entertainers	Radio and television announcers and newscasters	New stations will be licensed as cable television introduces more programming.
	Actors and actresses	Employment expected to grow faster than average, but field will be crowded.
Technologists and Technicians, Except Health	Drafters	Industrial growth and increasingly complex design problems will create a demand for drafters.
	Engineering and science technicians	More technicians will be needed to assist growing number of engineers and scientists.
	Legal assistants	Lawyers will employ more assistants for routine tasks.

Cluster	Occupation	Outlook/Advice
Technologists and Technicians, Except Health (continued)	Programmers	More computers will require more programmers.
	Technical writers	The need to communicate growing amount of scientific and technical information will create more openings for these professionals.
Marketing and Sales Occupations	Automobile sales workers	Demand for automobiles will increase.
	Real estate agents and brokers	Demand for housing and other properties will grow; field will be competitive, however.
	Securities sales workers	Economic growth and rising personal incomes will increase opportunities for investment.
	Travel agents	Employment expected to grow faster than average.
Administrative Support Occupations, Including Clerical	Bank clerks	Banking services will expand.
	Bank tellers	Same as above.
	Claims representatives	Insurance claims will increase.
	Computer operating personnel	Employment of console and peripheral equipment operators will rise as use of computers increases.
	Receptionists	Employment expected to grow faster than average as businesses expand.
	Secretaries	Field expected to grow faster than average, especially for part-time and temporary workers.
Food and Beverage Preparation and Service Occupations	Food counter workers	Job openings will be plentiful because of growing number of fast-food restaurants.
	Waiters' assistants and kitchen helpers	Increasing number of eating places will make many jobs available.

Cluster	Occupation	Outlook/Advice
Health Service Occupations	Dental assistants	Dentists will increasingly use chair-side assistants.
	Medical, occupational therapy, optometric, and physical therapy assistants	Specialists will meet the increasing demand for diversified health care by employing assistants.
Electrical and Electronic Equipment Repairers	Computer service technicians	As use of computer equipment grows, opportunities will be plentiful for people with postsecondary training in electronics.
	Television and radio service technicians	Growing popularity of in-home electronics equipment means this area will offer many jobs.
	Business machine repairers	Variety of business machines will increase affording more jobs.
Construction Jobs	Bricklayer, cement masons, drywall installers, and insulation workers	Favorable increase rates coupled with growing demand for family housing will mean boom times for these jobs.

Sources of State and Local Job Outlook Information

Your state maintains offices that monitor the job outlook in your state and region. Call or write agencies listed below for information about occupations.

Alabama

Chief, Research and Statistics Division
Department of Industrial Relations
Industrial Relations Building, Room 427
649 Munroe Street
Montgomery, AL 36130
(205) 261-5461

Director, Alabama Occupational Information
   Coordinating Committee
Bell Building, Suite 400
207 Montgomery Street
Montgomery, AL 36130
(205) 261-2990

Alaska

Chief, Research and Analysis Section
Alaska Department of Labor
P.O. Box 25501
Juneau, AK 99802
(907) 465-4500

Coordinator, Alaska Occupational Information Coordinating Committee
Alaska Department of Labor
P.O. Box 25501, Juneau, AK 99802
(907) 465-4518

Arizona

Research Administrator, Labor Market Information,
   Research and Analysis Section
Department of Economic Security
733-A, P.O. Box 6123
Phoenix, AZ 85005
(602) 255-3616

Arkansas

Chief, Research and Analysis Section
Employment Security Division
Arkansas Department of Labor
P.O. Box 2981, Little Rock, AR 77203
(501) 682-1544

Executive Director, Arkansas Occupational Information Coordinating
  Committee
Research and Analysis Section
Arkansas Employment Security Division
P.O. Box 2981, Little Rock, AR 72203
(501) 682-3159

California

Chief, Employment Data and Research Division
Employment Development Department
P.O. Box 942880
Sacramento, CA 94280
(916) 427-4675

Executive Director
California Occupational Information Coordinating Committee
800 Capitol Mall, MIC-67
Sacramento, CA 95814
(916) 323-6544

Colorado

Chief, Labor Market Information
Colorado Department of Labor and Employment
1330 Fox Street
Denver, CO 80204
(303) 620-4544

Director, Colorado Occupational Information Coordinating Committee
1391 North Spear Boulevard
Suite 600
Denver, CO 80204
(303) 866-4488

Connecticut

Director, Research and Information
Employment Security Division
Connecticut Labor Department
200 Folly Brook Boulevard
Wethersfield, CT 06109
(203) 566-2120

Executive Director, Connecticut Occupational Information
  Coordinating Committee
25 Industrial Park Road
Middletown, CT 06457
(203) 638-4042

Delaware

Chief, Office of Occupational and Labor Market Information
Delaware Department of Labor
P.O. Box 9029
Newark, DE 19714
(302) 368-6962

Chief, Office of Occupational and Labor Market Information
Delaware Department of Labor
University Office Plaza
P.O. Box 9029
Newark DE 19714
(302) 368-6962

District of Columbia

Chief, Division of Labor Market Information,
  Research and Analysis
District of Columbia Department of Employment Services
500 C Street NW, Room 411
Washington, DC 20001
(202) 639-1642

Executive Director, District of Columbia Occupational
  Information Coordinating Committee
Department of Employment Services
500 C Street NW
Washington, DC 20001
(202) 639-1083

Florida

Chief, Labor Market Information
Florida Department of Labor and Employment Security
2574 Seagate Drive, Suite 203
Tallahassee, FL 32399
(904) 488-1048

Director, Florida Occupational Information System
210 Atkins Building
1320 Executive Center Drive
Tallahassee, FL 32399
(904) 488-7397

Georgia

Director, Labor Information Systems
Georgia Department of Labor
254 Washington Street SW
Atlanta, GA 30334
(404) 656-3177

Executive Director, Georgia Occupational Information
   Coordinating Committee
Sussex Place, 148 International Boulevard NE
Atlanta, GA 30303
(404) 656-3177

Hawaii

Chief, Research and Statistics Office
Department of Labor and Industrial Relations
830 Punchbowl Street, Room 304
Honolulu, HI 96813
(808) 548-7639

Executive Director, Hawaii State Occupational Information
   Coordinating Committee
830 Punchbowl Street, Room 315
Honolulu, HI 96813
(808) 548-3496

Idaho

Chief, Research and Analysis
Idaho Department of Employment
317 Main Street
Boise, ID 83735
(208) 334-6168

Director, Idaho Occupational Information Coordinating Committee
Len B. Jordan Building, Room 301
650 West State Street
Boise, ID 83720
(208) 334-3705

Illinois

Director, Economic Information and Analysis Division
Illinois Department of Employment Security
401 South State Street, 2 South
Chicago, IL 60605
(312) 793-2316

Executive Director, Illinois Occupational Information
    Coordinating Committee
217 East Monroe, Suite 203
Springfield, IL 62706
(217) 785-0789

Indiana

Chief, Labor Market Information and Statistical Services
Indiana Employment Security Division
10 North Senate Avenue
Indianapolis, IN 46206
(317) 232-7701

Executive Director, Indiana Occupational Information
    Coordinating Committee
Indiana State Teachers' Association
50 West Market Street, 7th Floor
Indianapolis, IN 46204
(317) 232-8547

Iowa

Manager, Research and Statistics
Iowa Department of Job Service
1000 East Grand Avenue
Des Moines, IA 50319
(515) 281-8181

Executive Director, Iowa Occupational Information
  Coordinating Committee
200 East Grand Avenue
Des Moines, IA 50309
(515) 281-8076

Kansas

Chief, Research and Analysis
Kansas Department of Human Resources
401 Topeka Boulevard
Topeka, KS 66603
(913) 296-5058

Director, Kansas Occupational Information Coordinating
  Committee
401 Topeka Boulevard
Topeka, KS 66603
(913) 296-1865

Kentucky

Manager, Labor Market Research and Analysis Branch
Department for Employment Services
Cabinet for Human Resources
275 East Main Street
Frankfort, KY 40621
(502) 564-7976

Coordinator, Kentucky Occupational Information Coordinating
  Committee
275 East Main Street, 2 Center
Frankfort, KY 40621
(502) 564-4258

Louisiana

Director, Research and Statistics Section
Louisiana State Department of Labor
P.O. Box 94094, Capitol Station
1001 North 23rd Street
Baton Rouge, LA 70804
(504) 342-3140

Coordinator, Louisiana Occupational Information Coordinating
  Committee
P.O. Box 94094
Baton Rouge, LA 70804
(504) 342-5151

Maine

Director, Division of Research and Analysis
Bureau of Employment Security
Maine Department of Labor
20 Union Street
Augusta, ME 04330
(207) 289-2271

Executive Director, Maine Occupational Information
  Coordinating Committee
State House Station 71
Augusta, ME 04333
(207) 289-2331

Maryland

Director, Research and Analysis Division
Maryland Department of Economic and Employment Development
Employment Security Administration
1100 North Eutaw Street
Baltimore, MD 21201
(301) 333-5000

Executive Director, Maryland Occupational Information
  Coordinating Committee
Economic and Employment Development
1100 North Eutaw Street
Suite 720
Baltimore, MD 21201
(301) 333-5606

Massachusetts

Director, Job Market Research and Policy
Massachusetts Division of Employment Security
Charles F. Hurley Building
Government Center
Boston, MA 02114
(617) 727-6556

Director, Massachusetts Occupational Information Coordinating
  Committee
Massachusetts Division of Employment Security
Charles F. Hurley Building, 2nd Floor
Government Center
Boston, MA 02114
(617) 727-6718

Michigan

Director, Research and Statistics Division
Michigan Employment Security Commission
7310 Woodward Avenue
Detroit, MI 48202
(313) 876-5445

Executive Coordinator, Michigan Occupational Information
  Coordinating Committee
106 West Allegan
310 Hollister Building
Lansing, MI 48909
(517) 373-0363

Minnesota

Director, Research and Statistical Services Office
Minnesota Department of Jobs and Training
390 North Robert Street
St. Paul, MN 55101
(612) 296-6545

Director, Minnesota Occupational Information Coordinating
  Committee
Minnesota Department of Jobs and Training
690 American Center Building
150 Kellog Boulevard
St. Paul, MN 55101
(612) 296-2072

Mississippi

Chief, Labor Market Information Department
Mississippi Employment Security Commission
P.O. Box 1699
Jackson, MS 39215-1699
(601) 961-7424

Executive Director, Mississippi Occupational Information
   Coordinating Committee
1005 Sillers Building
P.O. Box 771
Jackson, MS 39205
(601) 359-3412

Missouri

Chief, Research and Analysis
Missouri Division of Employment Security
P.O. Box 59
Jefferson City, MO 65104
(314) 751-3591

Director, Missouri Occupational Information Coordinating
   Committee
421 East Dunklin Street
Jefferson City, MO 65101
(314) 751-3800

Montana

Chief, Research and Analysis
Department of Labor and Industry
P.O. Box 1728
Helena, MT 59624
(406) 444-2430

Program Manager, Montana Occupational Information
   Coordinating Committee
P.O. Box 1728
Helena, MT 59624
(406) 444-2741

Nebraska

Chief, Labor Market Information
Nebraska Department of Labor
P.O. Box 94600
Lincoln, NB 68509
(402) 475-8451

Administrator, Nebraska Occupational Information Coordinating
Committee
P.O. Box 94600, State House Station
Lincoln, NB 68509
(402) 471-4845

Nevada

Chief, Employment Security Research
Nevada Employment Security Department
500 East Third Street
Carson City, NV 89713
(702) 885-4550

Director, Nevada Occupational Information Coordinating
Committee
505 East King Street, Room 601
Carson City, NV 89710
(702) 885-4577

New Hampshire

Director, Economic Analysis and Reports
New Hampshire Department of Employment Security
32 South Main Street
Concord, NH 03301
(603) 224-3311

Director, New Hampshire State Occupational Information
Coordinating Committee
64-B Old Suncook Road
Concord, NH 03301
(603) 228-9500

New Jersey

Director, Division of Planning and Research
New Jersey Department of Labor
P.O. Box CN 056
Trenton, NJ 08625
(609) 272-2643

Staff Director, New Jersey Occupational Information
  Coordinating Committee
Labor and Industry Building
P.O. Box CN 056
Trenton, NJ 08625
(609) 292-2682

New Mexico

Chief, Economic Research and Analysis
Employment Security Department
P.O. Box 1928
Albuquerque, NM 87103
(505) 841-8647

Executive Director, New Mexico Occupational Information
  Coordinating Committee
Tiwa Building
401 Broadway NE
P.O. Box 1928
Albuquerque, NM 87103
(505) 841-8636

New York

Director, Division of Research and Statistics
New York State Department of Labor
State Campus, Building 12
Albany, NY 12240
(518) 457-6181

Executive Director, New York State Occupational Information
  Coordinating Committee
New York State Department of Labor
State Campus, Building 12
Albany, NY 12240
(518) 457-6182

North Carolina

Director, Labor Market Information Division
Employment Security Commission of North Carolina
P.O. Box 25903
Raleigh, NC 27611
(919) 733-2936

Director, North Carolina Occupational Information Coordinating
Committee
1311 St. Mary's Street, Suite 250
P.O. Box 27625
Raleigh, NC 27611
(919) 733-6700

North Dakota

Chief, Research and Statistics
Job Service North Dakota
P.O. Box 1537
Bismarck, ND 58502
(701) 224-2868

Director, North Dakota Occupational Information Coordinating
Committee
P.O. Box 1537
Bismarck, ND 58502
(701) 224-2733

Ohio

Director, Labor Market Information Division
Ohio Bureau of Employment Services
P.O. Box 1618
Columbus, OH 43216
(614) 644-2689

Director, Ohio Occupational Information Coordinating Committee
Division of Labor Market Information
Ohio Bureau of Employment Services
1160 Dublin Road, Building A
Columbus, OH 43215
(614) 644-2689

Oklahoma

Chief, Research and Planning Division
Oklahoma Employment Security Commission
310 Will Rodgers Memorial Office Building
Oklahoma City, OK 73105
(405) 557-7104

Director, Oklahoma State Department of Vocational and
  Technical Education
1500 West 7th Avenue
Stillwater, OK 74074
(405) 377-2000, ext. 268

Oregon

Administrator, Employment Division
Department of Human Resources
875 Union Street NE
Salem, OR 97311
(503) 378-3220

Executive Director, Oregon Occupational Information Coordinating
  Committee
875 Union Street NE
Salem, OR 97311
(503) 378-8146

Pennsylvania

Chief, Research and Statistics Division
Pennsylvania Department of Labor and Industry
7th and Forster Streets
Harrisburg, PA 17121
(717) 787-3265

Director, Pennsylvania Occupational Information Coordinating
  Committee
Governor's Office of Policy Development
506 Finance Building
P.O. Box 1323
Harrisburg, PA 17105
(717) 783-8384

Puerto Rico

Chief, Department of Labor and Human Resources
Bureau of Labor Statistics
505 Munoz Rivera Avenue, 17th Floor
Hato Rey, PR 00918
(809) 754-5339

Executive Director, Puerto Rico Occupational Information
  Coordinating Committee
P.O. Box 6212
San Juan, PR 00936
(809) 723-7110

Rhode Island

Supervisor, Employment Security Research
Rhode Island Department of Employment Security
24 Mason Street
Providence, RI 02903
(401) 277-3704

Director, Rhode Island Occupational Information Coordinating
  Committee
22 Hayes Street, Room 133
Providence, RI 02908
(401) 272-0830

South Carolina

Director, Labor Market Information Division
South Carolina Employment Security Commission
P.O. Box 995
Columbia, SC 29202
(803) 737-2660

Director, South Carolina Occupational Information Coordinating
  Committee
1550 Gadsden Street
P.O. Box 995
Columbia, SC 29202
(803) 737-2733

South Dakota

Chief, Labor Market Information Center
Department of Labor
P.O. Box 4730
Aberdeen, SD 57402
(605) 622-2314

Executive Director, South Dakota Occupational Information
  Coordinating Committee
Department of Labor
P.O. Box 4730
Aberdeen, SD 57402
(605) 622-2314

Tennessee

Chief, Research and Statistics
Tennessee Department of Employment Security
519 Cordell Hull Building
436 Sixth Avenue North
Nashville, TN 37219
(615) 741-2284

Director, Tennessee Occupational Information Coordinating Committee
519 Cordell Hull Building
436 Sixth Avenue North
Nashville, TN 37219
(615) 741-6451

Texas

Chief, Economic Research and Analysis
Texas Employment Commission
15th and Congress Avenue
Austin, TX 78778
(512) 463-2326

Director, Texas Occupational Information Coordinating Committee
TEC Building
15th and Congress Avenue, Room 526T
Austin, TX 78778
(512) 463-2399

Utah

Chief, Research and Analysis
Utah Department of Employment Security
P.O. Box 11249
Salt Lake City, UT 84147
(801) 533-2014

Director, Utah Occupational Information Coordinating Committee
174 Social Hall Avenue
P.O. Box 11249
Salt Lake City, UT 84147
(801) 533-2400

Vermont

Director, Policy and Information
Vermont Department of Employment and Training
P.O. Box 488
Montpelier, VT 05602
(802) 229-0311

Director, Vermont Occupational Information Coordinating Committee
Green Mountain Drive
P.O. Box 488
Montpelier, VT 05602
(802) 229-0311

Virginia

Director, Office of Research and Analysis
Virginia Employment Commission
P.O. Box 1358
Richmond, VA 23211
(804) 786-7496

Executive Director, Virginia Occupational Information
  Coordinating Committee
Virginia Employment Commission
P.O. Box 1358
703 East Main Street
Richmond, VA 23211
(804) 786-3177

Washington

Director, Labor Market and Economic Analysis Branch
Washington Employment Security Department
212 Maple Park, MS KG-11
Olympia, WA 98504
(206) 438-4800

Director, Washington State Occupational Information Coordinating
  Committee
212 Maple Park, MS KG-11
Olympia, WA 98504
(206) 438-4800

West Virginia

Chief, Division of Labor and Economic Research
Department of Employment Security
112 California Avenue
Charleston, WV 25305
(304) 348-2660

Executive Director, West Virginia Occupational Information
  Coordinating Committee
1600½ Washington Street
East Charleston, WV 25311
(304) 348-0061

Wisconsin

Chief, Labor Market Information Section
Department of Industry, Labor and Human Relations
P.O. Box 7944
Madison, WI 53707
(608) 266-5843

Executive Director, Wisconsin Occupational Information
  Coordinating Committee
Governor's Employment and Training Office
P.O. Box 7944
Madison, WI 53707
(608) 266-6722

Wyoming

Chief, Research and Analysis Section
Employment Security Commission
P.O. Box 2760
Casper, WY 82602
(307) 235-3642

Director, Wyoming Occupational Information Coordinating Committee
Occupational Information Program
Herschler Building, 2nd Floor E
Cheyenne, WY 82002
(307) 777-5837

6

How to Help
Your Child Explore
Careers

This chapter presents advice about how to explore careers arranged in a step-by-step format that you can follow with your child. As I explained in Chapter 1, the four keys to career planning are these: study yourself; become familiar with entry pathways to various occupations; review plans and progress with another person; test hypotheses and predictions about yourself in an occupation. Each of these is a major step in the process, under which come specific activities that you and your child can do.

Step 1: Study Yourself

As I pointed out in Chapter 3, certain factors and forces will influence the vocational choices your child will make: personality and behavior, abilities and aptitudes, interests, and educational preparation. If you haven't done so yet, here are several activities you should complete before reading on.

First Activity. Have your child review the careers listed by academic subject area in Chapter 3. Under the subject he or she is best at, your child should circle any careers that are appealing, then list them in column A.

Column A   **Column B**

_____   _____

_____   _____

_____   _____

_____   _____

_____   _____

Second Activity. On a separate piece of paper, have your child list leisure activities he or she enjoys. Use column B to list the kinds of work these activities suggest.

Third Activity. Next, summarize in a sentence any pattern that appears. For example, "The kind of work he likes involves mathematics and using his hands."

_____

_____

Step 2: Become Familiar with Entry Pathways to Various Occupations

The activities suggested above are the first informal steps in identifying your child's interests and abilities. Next, let's turn to a test or survey to supply us with additional information about your child.

First Activity. Arrange for your child to take the Armed Services Vocational Aptitude Battery (ASVAB) through a local recruiter or your child's guidance department. Remember that the test is free and there's no military obligation (see Chapter 4). An alternative is the Differential Aptitude Test (DAT), but scheduling the ASVAB is generally easier because military recruiters are located throughout the country. Write in column C your child's two or three strongest aptitudes based on the results of the test.

Column C   **Column D**

_____   _____

_____   _____

_____   _____

                                  _____

                                  _____

                                  _____

Second Activity. If it hasn't been done already, have your child complete the career interest survey at the end of Chapter 4. Then, in column D, he or she should list a representative sample of some of the career possibilities circled under each of the three occupational types in the highest scored areas. Compare aptitudes from column C with career possibilities in column D. But if there's no apparent pattern, don't be concerned; concentrate on the activities that follow.

Third Activity. Make an appointment to see your child's counselor and use the suggested list of questions for a counselor in Chapter 4. Bring along results from an aptitude test, a career interest survey (these may already be in your child's file), or the work you've done in this chapter. Double check that your child is taking courses and making educational plans that parallel her vocational interests.

Fourth Activity. After identifying interests and abilities and verifying that your child is enrolled in the right type of courses, move on to exploring specific occupations. Use the ones your child listed in column D above. As she learns about them, she might be drawn to other possibilities, as well.

At your school or local library, ask for assistance in locating and using any of the following resources for occupational information:

- _The Occupational Outlook Handbook_ is, in many professionals' opinion, the bible of occupational information. A survey conducted in the early 1980s showed that 92 percent of schools nationwide owned one or more copies. The _Handbook,_ published every two years by the U.S. Department of Labor, describes in detail about 200 occupations (about 3 of every 5 jobs in the economy). Although many occupations from the full spectrum of work are covered, generally those that require post-high-school training or are projected to grow rapidly receive the most attention. Each statement in the handbook follows a standard format, making it easier to compare jobs. Every profile of an occupation includes these subtopics: Nature of the Work; Working Conditions; Employment; Training, Other Qualifications, and Advancement; Job Outlook; Earnings; Related Occupations; and Sources of Additional Information. The *Handbook* also includes special features—"Tomorrow's Jobs: An Overview," for instance—which summarize trends and research noted in the *Handbook*'s companion magazine: *Occupational Outlook Quarterly.*

- *Career fiction* portrays one person or a group of people in a fictional work setting: the main character(s) might be nurses, or teachers, for example. Career fiction is usually high-interest reading, but authors sometimes overglamorize the profession they're describing.

- *Biographies* concentrate on a historical subject: the life of a famous scientist, for example. The descriptions of the person's career and the challenges he or she faced can provide glimpses of a particular field of endeavor.

- *Occupational monographs* treat one job thoroughly: its educational prerequisites, duties, salary, and characteristics it shares with similar kinds of work.

- *Occupational briefs,* on the other hand, give an overview of an occupational area, then summarize the various specializations within the field.

- *Occupational abstracts* give the most concise portrait of a particular job and explain the nature of the work in general terms.

- *Occupational guides* are often outlines, leaflets or, at most, booklets about a specific field. A typical title might be, "Your Career in Dentistry."

- *A job series* covers an occupational area, giving general information about all the job opportunities in the field. A number of book publishers offer extensive lists of titles in their job series.

- *Business and industrial descriptive literature* usually carry broad titles such as "The World of Insurance," and profile one business or industry.

- *Articles or reprints of articles* from newspapers, magazines, and journals are usually written in an informal style for a general audience. The "newsy" angle of most career-related articles is that the career being spotlighted has a promising outlook.

- *Community surveys, economic reports, and job analyses* are highly statistical, comprehensive reports of job trends in regions of the country. Most of the time, the information is too specific to help young job-seekers.

Fifth Activity. Explore sources of information beyond what's available in a library. Most *federal agencies* publish free information about occupations. Your child can request materials from:

U.S. Department of Agriculture—Forest Service
Personnel Management, Room 906 RP-E
P.O. Box 96090
Washington, DC 20090

U.S. Department of Agriculture—Office of Information
Special Programs Division, Room 536A
Washington, DC 20250

U.S. Department of Energy
Office of Scientific and Technical Information
P.O. Box 62
Oak Ridge, TN 37831

U.S. Department of Justice
Federal Bureau of Investigation Headquarters
10th and Pennsylvania Avenues
Washington, DC 20535

U.S. Department of Transportation
Federal Aviation Administration
Public Information Center, APA-230
800 Independence Avenue SW
Washington, DC 20591

U.S. Geological Survey
Geologic Inquiries Group
907 National Center
Reston, VA 22092

Professional, union, and industrial organizations also publish free information about careers, available on request. Your child might want to contact some of the organizations listed below:

Accounting

American Institute of Certified Public Accountants
1211 Avenue of the Americas
New York, NY 10036

American Accounting Association (AAA)
5717 Bessie Drive
Sarasota, FL 34233

Aerospace Engineering

American Institute of Aeronautics and Astronautics, Inc.
555 West 57th Street
New York, NY 10019

National Society of Professional Engineers
1420 King Street
Alexandria, VA 22314

Agriculture

Future Farmers of America
Attention: Career Information
P.O. Box 15160
Alexandria, VA 22309

U.S. Department of Agriculture
Extension Service
Washington, DC 20250

Allied Health Assisting and Technology

American Medical Association
Department of Allied Health Education and Accreditation
535 North Dearborn Street
Chicago, IL 60610

American Medical Technologists
710 Higgins Road
Park Ridge, IL 60068

American Association of Medical Assistants
20 North Wacker Drive, Suite 1576
Chicago, IL 60606

Allied Health Sciences

American Health Care Association
1200 15th Street NW
Washington, DC 20005

American Institute of Biological Sciences
730 11th Street NW
Washington, DC 20001

Anthropology

American Anthropological Association
1703 New Hampshire Avenue NW
Washington, DC 20009

Architecture

American Institute of Architecture Students (AIAS)
1735 New York Avenue NW
Washington, DC 20006

Art

American Artist Professional League (AAPL)
47 Fifth Avenue
New York, NY 10003

Astronomy

American Astronomical Society (AAS)
1816 Jefferson Place NW
Washington, DC 20009

Banking and Finance

American Bankers Association
Bank Personnel Division
1120 Connecticut Avenue NW
Washington, DC 20036

National Association of Bank Women
500 North Michigan Avenue, Suite 1400
Chicago, IL 60611

Biology

American Institute of Biological Sciences
730 11th Street NW
Washington, DC 20001

American Society for Microbiology
1913 Eye Street NW
Washington, DC 20006

Botany

American Society for Horticultural Science
701 North St. Asaph Street
Alexandria, VA 22314

Business Administration and Management

American Management Association
135 West 50th Street
New York, NY 10020

Association of MBA Executives, Inc.
AMBA Center
227 Commerce Street
East Haven, CT 06512

Chemical Engineering

American Institute of Chemical Engineers
345 East 47th Street
New York, NY 10017

National Society of Professional Engineers
1420 King Street
Alexandria, VA 22314

Chemistry

American Chemical Society
1155 16th Street NW
Washington, DC 20036

Chemist's Club
52 East 41st Street
New York, NY 10017

Civil Engineering

American Society of Civil Engineers
345 East 47th Street
New York, NY 10017

National Society of Professional Engineers
1420 King Street
Alexandria, VA 22314

Communications

International Communication Association
P.O. Box 9589
Austin, TX 78766

Women in Communications, Inc.
P.O. Box 9561
Austin, TX 78766

Computers

American Federation of Information Processing Societies
1899 Preston White Drive
Reston, VA 22091

American Society for Information Science
1424 16th Street NW, Suite 404
Washington, DC 20036

Association for Computer Professionals
230 Park Avenue
New York, NY 10169

Construction

Associated General Contractors of America, Inc.
1957 E Street NW
Washington, DC 20006

National Association of Home Builders
15th and M Streets NW
Washington, DC 20005

Culinary Arts

Culinary Institute of America
P.O. Box 53
Hyde Park, NY 12538

American Culinary Federation
P.O. Box 3466
St. Augustine, FL 32084

Educational Foundation of the National Restaurant Association (NRA)
20 North Wacker Drive, Suite 2620
Chicago, IL 60606

Economics

American Economic Association
1313 21st Avenue, S
Nashville, TN 37212

Foundation for Economic Education
30 South Broadway
Irvington, NY 10533

National Economist Club
P.O. Box 19281
Washington, DC 20036

Education

American Federation of Teachers
555 New Jersey Avenue NW
Washington, DC 20001

U.S. Department of Education
Center for Statistics
555 New Jersey Avenue NW
Washington, DC 20208

Electrical/Electronic Engineering

Institute of Electrical and Electronic Engineers
345 East 47th Street
New York, NY 10017

National Society of Professional Engineers
1420 King Street
Alexandria, VA 22314

Electrical/Electronics Technology

American Electronics Association
5201 Great America Parkway
Santa Clara, CA 95054

International Brotherhood of Electrical Workers
1125 15th Street NW
Washington, DC 20005

International Union of Electronic, Electrical, Salaried, Machine and
  Furniture Workers
1126 16th Street NW
Washington, DC 20036

English

American Society of Magazine Editors
575 Lexington Avenue, Suite 540
New York, NY 10022

Dow Jones Newspaper Fund
P.O. Box 300
Princeton, NJ 08543

National Council of Teachers of English
1111 Kenyon Road
Urbana, IL 61801

National Writers Club
1450 South Havana, Suite 620
Aurora, CO 80012

Food and Beverage Management/Service

National Restaurant Association
Information Service and Library
1200 17th Street NW
Washington, DC 20036

Educational Foundation of the National Restaurant Association (NRA)
20 North Wacker Drive, Suite 2620
Chicago, IL 60606

Foreign Language

Modern Language Association of America
10 Astor Place
New York, NY 10003

Association of Department of Foreign Languages
10 Astor Place
New York, NY 10003

American Institute for Foreign Study, Inc.
102 Greenwich Avenue
Greenwich, CT 06830

Forestry

American Forestry Association
1516 P Street NW
Washington, DC 20005

Society of American Foresters
5400 Grosvenor Lane
Bethesda, MD 20814

Society for Range Management
1839 York Street
Denver, CO 80206

U.S. Forest Service
U.S. Department of Agriculture
P.O. Box 96090
Washington, DC 20090

Geography

Association of American Geographers
1710 16th Street NW
Washington, DC 20009

Geology

Geological Society of America
P.O. Box 9140
3300 Penrose Place
Boulder, CO 80301

American Institute of Professional Geologists
7828 Vance Drive, Suite 103
Arvada, CO 80003

American Association of Petroleum Geologists
P.O. Box 979
Tulsa, OK 74101

Health Administration, Management, and Related Services

Association of University Programs in Health Administration
1911 North Fort Myer Drive, Suite 503
Arlington, VA 22209

American College of Health Care Administrators
8120 Woodmont Avenue, Suite 200
Bethesda, MD 20814

History

American Historical Association
400 A Street SE
Washington, DC 20003

Organization of American Historians
112 North Bryan Street
Bloomington, IN 47401

Home Economics

American Home Economics Association
2010 Massachusetts Avenue NW
Washington, DC 20036

The American Dietetic Association
208 South LaSalle, Suite 1100
Chicago, IL 60604

Horticulture

American Society for Horticultural Science
701 North St. Asaph Street
Alexandria, VA 22314

Society of American Florists
1601 Duke Street
Alexandria, VA 22314

Hotel/Motel Management

Council on Hotel, Restaurant and Institutional Education
1200 17th Street NW, 7th Floor
Washington, DC 20036

Industrial Engineering

Institute of Industrial Engineers, Inc.
25 Technology Park Atlanta
Norcross, GA 30092

National Society of Professional Engineers
1420 King Street
Alexandria, VA 22314

Industrial and Precision Production/Technology

National Tooling and Machining Association
9300 Livingston Road
Fort Washington, MD 20744

National Machine Tool Builders Association
7901 Westpart Drive
McLean, VA 22102

Law

American Bar Association
750 North Lake Shore Drive
Chicago, IL 60611

Association of American Law Schools
One Dupont Circle
Washington, DC 20036

Legal and Protective Services

National Association of Legal Assistants
1601 South Main, Suite 300
Tulsa, OK 74119

Library and Information Sciences

American Library Association
50 East Huron Street
Chicago, IL 60611

American Society for Information Science
1424 16th Street NW, Suite 404
Washington, DC 20036

Marketing and Distribution

American Marketing Association
250 South Wacker Drive, Suite 200
Chicago, IL 60606

Sales and Marketing Executives International
Statler Office Tower, Suite 458
Cleveland, OH 44115

Mathematics

American Mathematical Society
P.O. Box 6248
Providence, RI 02940

Mathematical Association of America
1529 18th Street NW
Washington, DC 20036

Association for Women in Mathematics
P.O. Box 178
Wellesley College
Wellesley, MA 02181

Mechanical Engineering

American Society of Mechanical Engineers
345 East 47th Street
New York, NY 10017

National Society of Professional Engineers
1420 King Street
Alexandria, VA 22314

Mechanics and Related Services

Automotive Service Industry Association
444 North Michigan Avenue
Chicago, IL 60611

Medicine and Dentistry

American Medical Association
535 North Dearborn Street
Chicago, IL 60610

American Osteopathic Association
142 East Ontario Street
Chicago, IL 60611

American Dental Association
211 East Chicago Avenue
Chicago, IL 60611

Metallurgical and Mining Engineering

American Society for Metals International
Metals Park, OH 44073

Metallurgical Society of AIME
420 Commonwealth Drive
Warrendale, PA 15086

National Society of Professional Engineers
1420 King Street
Alexandria, VA 22314

Military Science

See "Recruiting" in the Yellow Pages of your local telephone directory;
your child can contact the branch he or she is interested in.

Nursing and Related Services

National Student Nurses Association
555 West 57th Street, Suite 1325
New York, NY 10019

National League for Nursing
10 Columbus Circle
New York, NY 10019

American Physical Therapy Association
1111 North Fairfax Street
Alexandria, VA 22314

Performing Arts

Hispanic Institute for the Performing Arts
P.O. Box 32249
Washington, DC 20007

Philosophy

American Philosophical Association
University of Delaware
Newark, DE 19716

Physics

American Institute of Physics
335 East 45th Street
New York, NY 10017

Physiology

American Physiological Society
9650 Rockville Pike
Bethesda, MD 20814

Political Science

Academy of Political Science
2852 Broadway
New York, NY 10025

American Political Science Association
1527 New Hampshire Avenue NW
Washington, DC 20036

National Conference of Black Political Scientists
Department of Political Science
University of Illinois
Urbana, IL 61801

Women's Caucus for Political Science
c/o Diane Folks
University Plaza
Georgia State University
Atlanta, GA 30303

Psychology

American Psychological Association
1200 17th Street NW
Washington, DC 20036

Association of Black Psychologists
P.O. Box 55999
Washington, DC 20040

National Hispanic Psychological Association
Los Angeles County Department of Mental Health
2415 West Sixth Street
Los Angeles, CA 90057

Recreation and Leisure

American Camping Association
Bradford Woods
5000 State Road, 67 North
Martinsville, IN 46151

National Recreation and Park Association
Division of Professional Services
31010 Park Center Drive
Alexandria, VA 22302

American Alliance for Health, Physical Education, Recreation and Dance
1900 Association Drive
Reston, VA 22091

Religion and Theology

National Council of Churches
Professional Church Leadership, Room 710
475 Riverside Drive
New York, NY 10115

Secretarial Science

Professional Secretaries International
301 East Armour Blvd.
Kansas City, MO 64111–1299

Office Education Association
5454 Cleveland Avenue
Columbus, OH 43229

Social Work

National Association of Social Workers, Inc.
7981 Eastern Avenue
Silver Spring, MD 20910

Council on Social Work Education
1744 R Street NW
Washington, DC 20009

Sociology

American Sociological Association
1772 N Street, NW
Washington, DC 20036

Transportation

Air Transport Association of America
1709 New York Avenue NW
Washington, DC 20006

American Trucking Association
2200 Mill Road
Alexandria, VA 22314

Association of American Railroads
50 F Street NW
Washington, DC 20001

United Transportation Union
14600 Detroit Avenue
Cleveland, OH 44107

Zoology

American Association of Zoological Parks and Aquariums
Route 88
Oglebay Park
Wheeling, WV 26003

Private companies sometimes provide printed information about their services. Use the Yellow Pages of your local directory to pinpoint the types of companies in the field your child shows interest in; request copies of consumer information.

College and university placement offices maintain small libraries of books, pamphlets, articles, and audio-visual materials related to careers. Many offer computer-aided career searches. Call to make an appointment.

Periodicals, especially special-interest magazines, create a sense of community for readers interested in one particular activity or occupation. See the Appendix at the back of this book for titles of special-interest magazines.

Step 3: Test Hypotheses and Predictions About Yourself in an Occupation

Once your child has focused in on one or several occupations as a result of taking an interest survey and researching information, it's time to find out what a day on the job would actually be like.

First Activity. Read Chapter 7, "Creative Ways for Your Child to Find Career Directions." Job shadowing, a one-day visit to a work site, is the easiest experience to arrange; start with that, using the advice in Chapter 7.

Second Activity. Encourage your child to find a job in the preferred field of work, perhaps the same one tested as part of a job-shadowing experience. Read Chapter 8, "Getting the Most Out of a First Job."

Finally, at various points during your child's career exploration, it's a good idea to encourage him or her to review the situation.

Step 4: Review Plans and Progress with Another Person

"Another person" can, of course, be you. But remember this: your child will change. Two years ago, your daughter could dream of nothing but interior design and begged to attend a two-year trade school. Now she wants to enroll as an undeclared major at a four-year college. This isn't unusual. Adolescents are often spontaneous and impulsive; their ideas about "what to be" can be just as mercurial. In addition, this behavior illustrates an important aspect of finding a career: vocational development is really a stream of decisions. Arriving at the right job isn't as smooth as pulling into a station on a train. It's more like finding the right tool in a big hardware store: you have to go into the process with some notion of what you're looking for (identify interests), be willing to ask questions and weigh alternatives (test hypotheses), and then make a decision about the next step based on all the information available.

Now, your ego might smart a bit at this next suggestion, but if you want to give your child as much latitude as possible to discuss career alternatives *without* real or imagined expectations coming from you, encourage your son or daughter to talk with a favorite teacher, community leader, or adult friend of the family. Make sure to ask your child, rather than the adult involved, to summarize the conversation. In that way, you demonstrate respect for your child's ability to make plans for the future.

But perhaps it's making a decision that poses a problem for your child. What if, despite the amount of research you both have done, your child is still squarely on the fence when it comes to the future, still feels there are too many confusing options and unknowns. In that case, here's what you can do.

First Activity. Go back and glance at the listening techniques described in Chapter 1. It will be important for you to be a good listener as you attempt to help your child's thinking move forward.

Second Activity. Find time without distractions when you and your child can talk without interruptions. Thrashing out a career decision in front of the school counselor or at the dinner table with everyone chiming in isn't optimal. When the two of you have found some quiet time, ask your child to put her goal into a sentence, as in "I want to be an engineer."

Next, ask her to list all the alternatives: Take a fourth year of math. Not take a fourth year of math. Go to a two-year college for a year and transfer. Try not to let her bring up new dilemmas; the rule is *stick to achieving the goal.*

I want to be an engineer

Risk acceptable	Risk mostly acceptable	Risk Unacceptable
① Take a fourth year of math	Not take a fourth year of math	Take two years of math
② Find out about electives		Just take any elective I want
Apply directly to an undergraduate engineering program	Enroll in a two-year college and transfer	Declare another major and transfer into engineering if still interested.
③ Call a college with an engineering program and ask about transfers	Talk to a professional engineer and ask for advice	

Then have her put each alternative into one of three columns: Risk Acceptable, Risk Mostly Acceptable, Risk Completely Unacceptable. In other words, most alternatives involve some inconvenience or taking a chance. It's the question of degree that matters. Having divided up the alternatives this way, tell your child to eliminate everything in the Risk Completely Unacceptable column.

Next, have her rank all of the remaining alternatives. Assign 1 to the risk most preferred, all the way down to the one least preferred. Finally, help work out a simple plan, one that will accomplish as many steps toward achieving the goal as possible. Your child may act only on the three top-ranked risks or perhaps most of them. But make acting on them into a plan:

1. We'll find out what's covered in a fourth year of math.
2. We'll make an appointment with your counselor to talk about electives for next year.
3. We'll call a college with an engineering program and ask how they regard students who apply as transfers into engineering.

Set an approximate deadline for accomplishing the plan. This way both of you will share the feeling that progress is being made, that the goal is being worked on.

By identifying a goal, listing alternatives, making a plan, and setting a deadline, you can help your son or daughter move beyond exploring careers to making progress along the path toward the right one.

7

Creative Ways For Your Child To Find Career Directions

We've been talking a lot about the "fit" between your child and a career. Based on abilities, interests, and intelligence, certain careers come into view offering a good fit. Many of these become apparent through career interest surveys, research, and reviewing a child's background. But up to this point, we're still window-shopping. A lot of occupations can look good—surgeon, test pilot, fashion model—but will your child also enjoy the mundane side of most occupations? I was talking recently to a high school friend of mine who's a policeman in our town. He's well-known and well-liked, and judging from his adolescent experiences as an athlete and an out-going person, it would seem that being a policeman would be just right for him.

"Being a police officer is great, but there are times when it's like being a garbageman, too," he said. *A garbageman?* "Sure, because we spend a lot of time going around town looking for the few people who constantly get into trouble—the ones who steal things, or vandalize buildings, or just hang around waiting for something to happen. We pick them up and take them home or take them to jail. We get stuck doing the jobs that have to be done."

Interesting, and not at all like the life of police portrayed on TV!

But how can we give children slice-of-life experiences, ones that will illustrate the light and dark sides of an occupation, when so many jobs require years of education or training? There are creative ways to find career directions, ways that supplement and enhance what a career interest survey indicates. These include volunteer work, job shadowing, internships, summer programs on college campuses, and study abroad programs. By participating in one of these, a child can get "hands-on" time at a job and see whether it's what he or she expected.

Volunteers Needed

Young people tend to divide work into two categories—paid and un-paid—and then put down the latter as not as valuable. But as adults, we know that volunteer work is an integral part of working in general and it's highly regarded. Many large businesses encourage their employees to become involved in civic activities. Also, especially in the business world, employees are expected to volunteer for committees, stay late on projects, or attend social events, all of it without additional pay.

Moreover, young career-seekers should know that having performed volunteer work is seen by many people as a sign of maturity or genuine interest in a field. College applications routinely ask applicants whether they have been involved in community activities; likewise, books offering advice to medical and law school applicants strongly encourage them to do volunteer work in any area of the profession as a prerequisite to applying for admission.

There are also psychic benefits from volunteer work: feelings of personal satisfaction for having pitched in. For example, Tina Anton, 17, was recruited by a friend to volunteer at a suburban Chicago youth shelter. After some training, she was assigned as a peer counselor in the Drop-In Center, the first stop for many clients who are on the run. "Working as a peer counselor I can have a direct effect on these teens," said Anton. "I can make a difference, let them know they are not alone, that there is someone to help."

Most important, of course, volunteer experiences can help your child refine career plans. Candystripers often become nurses or doctors; hotline assistants sometimes become social workers, counselors, or psychologists. Volunteer experiences can be the turning point in a young person's career thinking.

Where can your child find opportunities to volunteer? Here are some agencies, organizations, and institutions that are always looking for an extra hand. Look in the Yellow Pages under "Social Service" for addresses and phone numbers:

Adult day care centers
Alcohol and family counseling
 centers
Blood drive programs
Botanical gardens
Community centers
Child abuse prevention centers
Community theater groups
Crisis hotlines
Environmental groups
Family and mental health
 services
Food collection agencies
Hospitals

Libraries
Migrant councils
Missions
Park and recreation programs
Political campaigns
Recordings for the blind
Recycling centers
The Salvation Army
United Way
Vocational services
YMCA/YWCA
The zoo

Should your child decide to perform some volunteer work, it would be a good idea for her to get a letter of recommendation from her supervisor when the stint is completed. A letter like this can make a persuasive addition to a college application, or be useful in lining up other work opportunities.

But one thing your child should keep in mind is this: *don't overcommit.* Young people sometimes have a hard time saying no to requests for more participation. The young person who spends too much time volunteering will feel embarrassed when he has to renege on previously agreed-to commitments because of falling grades, for example. As Sabrina McMathis, 18, youth research assistant for the Youth Services Department of the Sheriff of Cook County advises, "Being a volunteer can bring a sense of fulfillment. It can give you a feeling of being wanted and needed. Volunteering, like a real employment opportunity, should be taken seriously—show the utmost responsibility."

Job Shadowing

"Walk a mile in my shoes," was the refrain of a popular song in the late sixties about understanding other people better. The closest your child can get to walking around in the shoes of an architect, a computer programmer, or a carpenter, for instance, is through job shadowing.

If you think about it, the idea isn't new. A long time ago, when people's businesses were located in full view of their neighbors (the blacksmith, the tanner, the miller, the tailor), children grew up witnessing what many adults did for a living. Undoubtedly, a lot of career decisions were based on first-hand observation (though circumstances played a greater role in determining people's vocations in those days). Today, however, most workers commute to their jobs or work in look-alike offices. Consequently, many young people are unaware of what adults do for a living like, for instance, the child of a businessman who thought her dad was a pilot because she and her mom took him to the airport so often.

To arrange a job shadowing day you might consider looking no farther than your own family. It surprises me how often I hear teenagers say that they don't know what their parents do for a living: "Oh, he works downtown for some big company." "She works for a doctor—something with patients." Invite your child to accompany you one day. Make sure you have one or several things ready that your child can do: filing, answering phones, going out on deliveries, or accompanying you on a sales call. Explain the ground rules in advance: how to dress, what to bring, what he'll be expected to do. You may be pleased to find out that your child comes away very impressed by your abilities. As one boy wrote on an evaluation sheet I gave him after spending the day with his dad in an electronics firm, "My dad has to make a lot of quick decisions. It's a high pressure job. I didn't know he knew so much about electronics and getting people to work together."

A second alternative is to arrange a pairing between your child and someone doing the kind of work that interests him. First, look around your circle of friends for a candidate. If no one fits the job description, then contact any of the following organizations, all of which have experience with schools and schoolchildren through Career Days and providing classroom speakers:

Chamber of Commerce	Optimist Club
Jaycees	Rotary International
Kiwanis Club	Sertoma Club
Lions Club	Any business large enough to have a public relations department

Ask to speak to an officer of the club or the person in charge of community relations. Give your name, phone number, and explain that your son or daughter would like to spend a day accompanying a certain type of worker—be specific. I find that using the term *job shadowing* gives people an immediate idea of what's being requested. Assure the person that you will provide transportation. Get the name of the person you're speaking to; if you don't hear anything in a week, call back. You might feel a little trepidation about making a cold call to someone you don't know and asking whether your child can come for a visit. But in the years that I've been arranging job shadowing days, *no one has turned me down.* Just think if someone called you and requested something similar: you'd probably be flattered.

On the day that your child is to make the visit, assign him a little research. Have him find out the answers to these questions:

1. What led to your being given this position?
2. How much training or education is necessary?
3. What are your responsibilities?
4. What do you like best about the work?
5. Are there any drawbacks?
6. What advice would you have for a person considering this kind of work?

Afterward, discuss your child's experiences with her. Ask her what she did and saw, whom she spoke to, what kind of work, if any, she was given to do, and what her overall impressions were. Try not to intimate that your child should make a career decision based on one day's activities. Remember, there is no day of reckoning or deadline when it comes to career planning, but all constructive activities are ultimately useful. As a way of encouraging businesslike behavior, have your child send a thank-you note.

Arranging an Internship

For young adults with a pretty firm idea of the career they'd like to pursue, an internship is a rung up the ladder from volunteer work and job shadowing.

The emphasis in an internship is on extended career development—learning what an employment area is really like over a significant period of time and deciding whether the intern is suited for the work. Unlike cooperative education programs, which are traditionally arranged through schools and colleges with businesses, internships can be in practically any career field. They may be salaried or nonsalaried, undertaken for credit or just for the experience. To give you an idea in a nutshell of what an internship can offer, this is what a listing might look like in a directory of internships.

Allstate Public Television, 1 Main Street, Centerville, MN 00001. Contact: Production Manager. Statewide community public television network incorporated November 1964.

Internships: Internship (nonsalaried) includes experience in camera operation, floor directing, lighting, audio, teleprompter, character generator, video switching, set construction, both studio and remote productions. Internship usually runs for a semester, but can run longer or shorter depending on student and school. College credit may be arranged. Possibility of future full-time employment.

Eligibility: Available to students who are residents of Minnesota or students of Minnesota schools. If space is available, out-of-state students will be accepted. Approximately 95 applications received each year; 8–12 candidates accepted each semester.

Application procedure: No formal deadline. Applicants are advised to apply early.

The best directory of internships available is *1988 Internships* (Writer's Digest Books, 1507 Dana Avenue, Cincinnati, OH 45207). This annual publication lists over 38,000 internships in areas such as publishing, newspapers, law and criminal justice, science and research, and other fields. Many libraries carry this book, or you can order it from the publisher. On the other hand, you and your child may prefer to arrange for a local internship, and save money that might have been spent relocating. To do this, consult these sources for the names and addresses of businesses or organizations in your child's area of interest:

The United Way

The Chamber of Commerce

The Yellow Pages

Career planning and placement offices at local colleges

Temporary job services

Business, professional, trade, or educational directories of organizations, including: *Standard and Poor's Register of Corporations, Directors, and Executives;* Dun & Bradstreet's *Million Dollar Directory* and *Dun & Bradstreet Ref-*

erence Book of Corporate Management; Moody's Complete Corporate Index; the *Encyclopedia of Associations;* and the *Career Guide to Professional Associations.*

Once your child targets a few possibilities, the approach to arranging an internship will have to be more sophisticated than arranging for volunteer work or a job shadowing day. Most employers consider interns normal employees, so your child should include some self-promotion, just as if he or she were job-hunting. Objectives should be stated clearly and succinctly: not "I want to work in an office environment" but instead, "I want to learn to put into practice principles of cost accounting, tax preparation, and budget management." Your child should spell out these objectives in a cover letter, and should also include a résumé emphasizing his or her education or abilities in the field. (See samples on pages 112 and 113.) See Chapter 8 for interviewing tips, should an interview be offered.

An internship can pave the way to employment with the same organization, or it can give your child a competitive edge when job-hunting. In any case, it will serve as a major stepping stone in his or her career exploration.

Summer Programs on College Campuses

Suppose your child could take a college for a "test drive"—not just going on a one-hour tour of the campus, or spending the weekend with a friend who's already enrolled, but actually being able to attend classes, live in the dormitories, socialize with other students, and tackle college-level work. And what if your child could enroll in career-related classes that would give a taste of the education required in the field, say, music, dance, engineering, environmental studies, or biology, for example? And perhaps best of all, imagine all this costing your family a fraction of what you'd be required to pay if your son or daughter were a fully enrolled freshman.

All this is possible through participation in an on-campus summer program for high school students. These programs have multiplied tremendously over the past few years, partly because parents and students are looking for ways to investigate colleges before committing thousands of dollars in tuition to a particular institution. As a result, many campuses in recent years have begun publicizing special science programs, fine arts workshops, writing seminars, drama productions, computer

Sample Cover Letter

David Simpson
124 Warwick
Park Forest, WI 18934

Mr. James Larson, Manager
COMPUTER LEARNING SYSTEMS
1435 Southdale Avenue, Suite 501
Moraine, WI 18973

Dear Mr. Larson:

I am writing about an internship opportunity with your firm. According to the research I've done at my college placement office, COMPUTER LEARNING SYSTEMS has previously offered internships to college students.

I am a sophomore at Cardinal Stritch College in Milwaukee where I'm majoring in computer programming. As you will be able to see from the enclosed résumé, I have had some experience working with computers on a part-time basis, but I'm anxious to see whether the field is really for me. Moreover, I've had enough course work that I believe I can perform capably in many professional situations involving computer programming.

My goals for an internship would be: to write programs for assigned projects or clients; to write proposals for new projects; to learn about new hardware and software available for education program-writing.

I will be contacting you in two weeks to arrange for an appointment to discuss a possible internship, unless you find time to call first. I look forward to hearing from you.

Sincerely,

David Simpson

Enclosure

Sample Résumé

```
                   DAVID SIMPSON
                    124 Warwick
                 Park Forest, WI 18934
                   (202) 555-1547

INTERNSHIP OBJECTIVE:   Seeking an internship in com-
                        puter programming where use
                        can be made of my skills and
                        where I can get practical ex-
                        perience working in the
                        field.

EDUCATION:              Bachelor of Science, Cardinal
                        Stritch College
                        Anticipated Graduation Date:
                        June, 1990
                        Major: Computer Science
                        Minor: Economics

WORK EXPERIENCE:        Dispatcher Ace Trucking, Inc.
                        Responsible for arranging
                        work schedules and communi-
                        cating with drivers on their
                        daily deliveries.
                        June—September, 1986

                        Consultant John Markham In-
                        surance Agency. Advised
                        client about various systems
                        worth purchasing to computer-
                        ize his office, then wrote
                        programs, putting all of his
                        clients on computer-accessi-
                        ble files.
                        November 1987—June 1988

HONORS/ACTIVITIES:      David A. Robinson Humanitar-
                        ian Award (high school)
                        Dean's List, two semesters at
                        college
                        Member of Keyboard Club

REFERENCES:             Available upon request
```

113

camps, classes for gifted students, and much more. The idea is to give high school students a taste of actually being at college. Take the experience of high school senior Liz Harder, for example, who attended the summer writing program at Carleton College in Northfield, Minnesota:

> I like writing, in fact I'm thinking of a career in writing, and I was interested in Carleton too, so I thought the summer program would fit right in. But as we were driving up there I started thinking, "Maybe I'm rushing things—maybe I just should've stayed home," all the usual last-minute thoughts. But I had no problems once we arrived.
>
> There were 105 kids from all over: Georgia, Montana, Hawaii, and Mexico, for instance. We met in the lounge and then we went to a lecture hall for orientation. All of our instructors were introduced to us. Then we were broken up into groups that would rotate between going to class, attending workshops, and participating in writing critiques. We had to stay up late a lot and the pace was fast, but experiencing that independence and meeting so many different people was great. It was the best experience of my life, and I've been on school trips abroad, too.

Besides the glimpses of college life that summer programs give students, there are concrete benefits to be had in terms of eventually applying to college, as well. Carol Lunkenheimer, Director of Admissions at Northwestern University in Evanston, Illinois, finds that admission committees not only look favorably on an applicant who has participated in a summer program, but also, "the experience carries more weight if it's related to a field that the student is considering—for example, a potential journalism major attending a summer journalism program. But in any case, it's a good introduction to time management and college-level work, and admission committees recognize this."

One other benefit of attending a summer program has to do with how your child's outlook about the future will change after having experienced higher education. As Dean Flora Davidson, Director of the precollege program at Barnard College, Columbia University, said, "It gives students an opportunity to test the academic rigor of college—forces them to make independent choices."

Choosing a Summer Program

There are three main points to keep in mind when comparing summer programs: Cost, location, and potential for personal growth.

Cost. Costs of summer programs span quite a range: from free to over $1,500. But differences in cost do not indicate differences in quality. Many times it's the nature of the activities that set the price. For example, a three-week art workshop that includes field trips, lectures, and materials has more built-in costs for the college than a three-week computer camp where all the participants are offered time in the college's computer lab. But either one can be just as satisfying, depending on what your child is looking for. So in the long run, the program's content will have more to do with whether you and your child think the experience is worthwhile than its cost.

But let's be realistic; few families are in a position to ignore the cost factor. If the price is a problem, you have two alternatives. The first is to find out whether the college offers financial aid to summer students. Occasionally, opportunities to apply for aid will be described along with other information about the program, as in the case of Harvard University's "Career Discovery at the Graduate School of Design." Under *Expenses* you'll find, "Financial aid for tuition is limited. Partial funding (up to 50 percent of tuition) based on need is available to a few applicants." But even if financial aid isn't mentioned in the program description, don't give up. Sometimes if a student indicates a sincere interest in attending, the funds will be made available: a tuition waiver is one possibility. The best method for pursuing this is for your child to get the name of the program's director or coordinator and write a letter of inquiry (see the sample letter on page 116).

Your second alternative for finding financial aid is to approach civic groups for help. In your community are service groups—Rotary, Kiwanis, or Jaycees, for instance—that maintain funds expressly for helping people reach worthwhile goals. Naturally, these groups are careful about how they manage their funds, so your child should arrange to appear at one of their meetings and make a presentation. Community service organizations are nearby, so there's no reason why the appeal shouldn't be made in person. This approach is more likely to be effective. During the presentation it will be important for your child to say:

Why he/she wants to attend the program
How it fits in with his/her long-range goals
What other methods of financing his/her way your family has planned

Whatever the outcome of the presentation, your child should send a thank-you note.

Location. One aspect of cost has to do with the distance of the pro-

Sample Letter of Inquiry

Mr. Jack Trent, Coordinator
Summer Program
College-on-the-Hill
Scholartown, MA 00155

Dear Mr. Trent:

I'm a junior at Urbana High School in Bedford Falls,
Ohio, who's planning to major in math at college.
One of the institutions I'm seriously considering is
College-on-the-Hill, so I was excited to discover
that you offer a summer program in college-level
math for high school students.

But my problem is this: the program cost is out of
my parents' reach. I plan to help with the expense
by working part time and I'm also going to approach
local civic groups for aid, but I still might not be
able to afford to attend. Is there some way you can
help me?

I'm including a copy of my high school transcript as
a way of indicating my interest in mathematics (you
can see my grades are good), and I'm also sending a
recommendation from my counselor. I hope this information will convince you of my sincere desire to attend the summer program. Please contact me at your
earliest convenience about whether I can hope for
some assistance.

Very truly yours,

gram from your home. Having to fly there, for example, is going to increase the overall cost, so be sure to add in transportation costs to your estimates. Of course the educational value of a program might make the extra expense worthwhile. The location of the school has a lot to do with the quality of the program: a workshop on forest ecology should be on a campus surrounded by forests.

One other thing about distance: it's not unusual for young people to feel some anxiety about being away from home. Let's face it, home-sickness is something that most of us have felt at one time or another, so the prospect of being on a college campus for a couple of weeks or perhaps even a month is bound to inspire some thoughts about whether your child will get along with strangers, etc. But look at it this way: if your child is college bound, it's possible he's going to go *away* to college eventually. In my experience as a counselor, one of the big selling points of an on-campus summer program is that it gives students the opportunity to test the waters of higher education. For a short while, your child will have the chance to be an undergraduate—and she'll probably find herself growing into the role.

Potential for personal growth. Your youngster is looking for an experience beyond the type that can be had in high school. A summer program gives young people the chance to spread their wings a little and accept challenges not likely to be offered at home. So encourage your child to shoot for programs that sound hard at first—these are the ones that are definitely worth the trouble to attend. Not only will she be a better student as a result, but she'll know that she is equal to handling the academic demands that college and her future career will make on her.

On-Campus Opportunities

Here is a list of some of the summer programs available. Some colleges offer more than one program.

Arkansas

Design Summer Workshop
Architecture and Landscape Architecture
Division of Continuing Education
#2 University Center
University of Arkansas
Fayetteville, AR 72701
(501) 575-3805

California

The Junior Statesman Summer School [at Stanford University]
The Junior Statesman Foundation
650 Bair Island, Suite 201
Redwood City, CA 94063
(800) 334-5353
(415) 366-2700 in Northern California

Summer Session
University of California at Berkeley
Berkeley, CA 94720
(415) 642-5611

Summer Discovery at UCLA

Eastern USA:
55 Bryant Avenue
Roslyn Village, NY 11576

Western USA:
310 DeNeve Drive, 163C Rieber Hall UCLA
Los Angeles, CA 90024

(516) 621-3939 for both

Summer Session
Mail Code X-004
University of California at San Diego
La Jolla, CA 92093
(619) 534-4364

Colorado

Summer Field Course
Energy Resources—Today and Tomorrow
Director of Student Life
Colorado School of Mines
Golden, CO 80401
(303) 272-3234

Young Scholars Summer Session
Farrand Hall
Campus Box 100
University of Colorado
Boulder, CO 80310
(303) 492-6694

Summer Enrichment Program
University of Northern Colorado
Greeley, CO 80639
(303) 351-2683

Connecticut

Connecticut College Summer Campus
Connecticut College
New London, CT 06320
(203) 447-7566

Yale University
Yale Summer Programs 1988 [or current year]
53 Wall Street, Dept. HS
P.O. Box 2145
New Haven, CT 06520
(203) 432-2430

District of Columbia

The American University Summer College
The American University
4400 Massachusetts Avenue NW
Washington, DC 20016
(202) 686-2845

The Junior Statesman Summer School [at Georgetown University]
The Junior Statesman Foundation
650 Bair Island Road, Suite 201
Redwood City, CA 94063
(800) 334-5353
(415) 366-2700 in Northern California

School for Summer and Continuing Education
Georgetown University
Washington, DC 20057
(202) 625-8106

   Summer College for High School Juniors

   College Prep Workshops in English and Math

   International Relations Program

Illinois

Manufacturing Engineering or
  Computerized Music Programs
Program Coordinator
Enrichment Program
146 Haussler Hall
Bradley University
Peoria, IL 61625

Columbia College
Summer Institute
600 South Michigan Avenue
Chicago, IL 60605-1996
(312) 663-1600

Eastern Illinois University
Office of Continuing Education
Booth House
Charleston, IL 61920

  Spanish Summer Camp for High School Students

  Summer Science Camp for High School Students

  Summer Leadership and College Prep Camp for Minority
    High School Students

Women in Science and Engineering:
Summer Program for High School Girls
IIT Center
Illinois Institute of Technology
Chicago, IL 60616-3793
(312) 567-3025

Summer Academy
College of Continuing Education and Public Service
Illinois State University
Normal, IL 61761
(309) 483-8691

National High School Institute
Northwestern University
2299 Sheridan Road
Evanston, IL 60201

Summer Junior Program
Saint Xavier College
3700 West 103rd Street
Chicago, IL 60655
(312) 779-3300, Ext. 281

Mississippi Valley Writing Project—Writing Camp for Kids
Director, MVWP
Southern Illinois University at Edwardsville
Box 1049
Edwardsville, IL 62026

Junior Engineering Technical Society Summer Programs
State of Illinois JETS Headquarters
207 Engineering Hall
University of Illinois at Urbana-Champaign
1308 West Green Street
Urbana, IL 61801

Mathematics Camps for Gifted High School Students
Conferences and Institutes
116 Illini Hall
725 South Wright Street
University of Illinois at Urbana-Champaign
Champaign, IL 61820
(217) 333-2881

University of Illinois/University High Summer Camp
Academic Summer Camps
1212 West Springfield
Urbana, IL 61801

School of Continuing Education
Sherman Hall 317
Western Illinois University
Macomb, IL 61455
(309) 298-1911
(800) 322-3902 in Illinois

  Youth Conservation Workshop

  High Adventure Camp

Indiana

Summer Workshops for High School Students in Computer Science
Department of Computer Science
Ball State University
Muncie, IN 47306-1099

Summer Programs for High School Juniors
Office of Admissions
Ball State University
Muncie, IN 47306-1099

Explore-a-College
Summer Programs
Box 23
Earlham College
Richmond, IN 47374
(317) 962-6561

High School Philosophy Institute
Department of Philosophy
Indiana University Bloomington
Sycamore Hall 026
Bloomington, IN 47405
(812) 335-9503

Office of Summer Sessions
Maxwell Hall, Department B
Indiana University Bloomington
Bloomington, IN 47405
(812) 335-0661

Summer Engineering Seminar
Freshman Engineering
Purdue University
West Lafayette, IN 47907
(317) 494-1776

Golf, Tennis and Sports
Information/Public Relations Camps
Purdue University
Mackey Arena
West Lafayette, IN 47907

Summer Residential Program for High-Ability Youth
Gifted Education Resource Institute
South Campus Courts—Building G
Purdue University
West Lafayette, IN 47907

Career Discovery Program in Architecture
School of Architecture
Purdue University
Notre Dame, IN 46556
(219) 239-7505

Introduction to Engineering for Women
College of Engineering
University of Notre Dame
Notre Dame, IN 46556

College Horizons Summer Camp
Camp Coordinator
Valparaiso University
Valparaiso, IN 46383-9978
(800) 348-2611 outside Indiana
(219) 464-5011

Summer Scholars Program
Community Services Center/32
Vincennes University
Vincennes, IN 47591
(800) 742-9198

Iowa

Office of Summer Programs
P.O. Box 805
Grinnell College
Grinnell, IA 50112-0810
(515) 236-2100

Engineering Honors Workshops
Iowa State University
Office of the Dean
College of Engineering
104 Marston Hall
Ames, IA 50011
(515) 294-5933

Summer Exploration of the Environment in Dubuque
Director of SEED Program
University of Dubuque
Dubuque, IA 52001

Secondary Student Training Program
Research Participation Program
455 Van Allen Hall
University of Iowa
Iowa City, IA 52242

Summer Youth Programs
University of Iowa
Office of Admissions
Calvin Hall
Iowa City, IA 52242
(319) 335-3847

Kansas

Summer Camps and Institutes
University of Kansas
Lawrence, KS 66045
(913) 864-4422

Kansas Writing Project—Summer Writing Camp
Department of English
Wichita State University
Wichita, KS 67208

Maryland

Center for the Advancement of Academically Talented Youth
Johns Hopkins University
Baltimore, MD 21218
(301) 338-8427

Massachusetts

The Boston College Experience Summer Session
Boston College
Chestnut Hill, MA 02167
(617) 552-3100

Summer Performance Program
Berklee College of Music
1140 Boylston Street
Boston, MA 02215
(617) 266-1400

Summer Studies in Mathematics
Hampshire College
Box SS
Amherst, MA 01002
(413) 549-4600, Ext. 357

Harvard University Secondary School Students Program
20 Garden Street
Harvard University
Cambridge, MA 02138

MIT MITES (Minority Introduction to Engineering and Science)
Director, MIT MITES
Massachusetts Institute of Technology
Room 3-108
77 Massachusetts Avenue
Cambridge, MA 02139
(617) 253-1415

Summermath
302 Shattuck Hall
Mount Holyoke College
South Hadley, MA 01075
(413) 538-2608

Focus at Tufts
P.O. Box 4
Tufts University
Medford, MA 02155
(617) 625-4850

Exploration Summer Program
124 High Rock Lane
Wellesley College
Westwood, MA 02090
(617) 329-4488

Michigan

Gail Warnaar Double Reed Camp
Hope College
Holland, MI 49423

Summer Youth Program
Michigan Technological University
Houghton, MI 49931
(906) 487-2219

Women in Engineering Program
Division of Education and Public Services
Michigan Technological University
Houghton, MI 49931
(906) 487-2219

Honors Summer Institute
1210 Angell Hall
University of Michigan
Ann Arbor, MI 48109-1003
(313) 764-6272

Engineering Exploration for High School Women
Society of Women Engineers
1226 EECS Building
University of Michigan
Ann Arbor, MI 48109

Minnesota

Twin City Institute for Talented Youth
Macalester College
1600 Grand Avenue
St. Paul, MN 55105
(612) 696-6590

Secondary School Summer Session
Moorhead State University
Moorhead, MN 56560
(218) 236-2762

Missouri

Career Institute for High School Juniors
St. Louis College of Pharmacy
Admissions Department
4588 Parkview Place
St. Louis, MO 63110
(314) 367-8700

Stephens College/Perry-Mansfield School and Camp at
  Steamboat Springs, Colorado
Box 2087
Columbia, MO 65215
(314) 876-7160

Architecture Discovery Program
School of Architecture
Campus Box 1079
Washington University
St. Louis, MO 63130
(314) 889-6200

New Hampshire

Summer Learning
University of New Hampshire
Education Department, Morrill Hall
Durham, NH 03824
(603) 862-2311

New Jersey

Rutgers University: University College—Camden
Rutgers Dean's Summer Scholars Program
University College—Camden
329 Cooper Street
Camden, NJ 08102
(609) 757-6098

New York

Summer in New York
Barnard's Pre-College Program
Dean Flora Davidson
Office of Special Academic Programs
Barnard College/Columbia University
3009 Broadway
New York, NY 10027-6598
(212) 280-8866

Cornell University Summer College
Box 85
B12 Ives Hall
Ithaca, NY 14853-3901
(607) 255-6203

PASS
Skidmore College
Sarasota Springs, NY 12866
(518) 584-5000 Ext. 2264

St. Lawrence University Summer Program
Canton, NY 13617
(315) 379-5991

The College Experience
Wells House
Union College
1 Union Avenue
Schenectady, NY 12308
(518) 370-6288

North Carolina

School for Gifted Students in the Arts
Brevard College
Brevard, NC 28712
(704) 883-8292, Ext. 212

Pre-College Program
01 West Duke Building
Duke University
Durham, NC 27708
(919) 684-3847

Ohio

Women in Engineering Program
School of Engineering
University of Dayton
Dayton, OH 45469-0001
(513) 229-4411

Oregon

Summer Enrichment Program for Talented and Gifted Students
University of Oregon
Eugene, OR 97403
(503) 686-5521

Pennsylvania

Pre-College Program in the Fine Arts
Director of Summer Studies
Summer Studies Office
Carnegie Mellon University
5000 Forbes Avenue.
Pittsburgh, PA 15213
(412) 578-6620

Pennsylvania Writing Project—Youth Writing Project
West Chester University of Pennsylvania
West Chester, PA 19383

Pre-College Program
University of Pennsylvania
210 Logan Hall
Philadelphia, PA 19104
(215) 898-3526

Rhode Island

Summer College
Brown University
Box 1920
Providence, RI 02912
(401) 863-2785

Career Explorations
Johnson & Wales College
Abbott Park Place
Providence, RI 02903

Texas

College Preparatory Institute
Southern Methodist University
Dallas, TX 75275
(214) 692-2981

Vermont

Bennington July Program
Bennington College
Bennington, VT 05201
(802) 442-5401

Virginia

Hollinsummer Pre-College Program
Coordinator of Summer Programs
Hollins College
P.O. Box 9694
Roanoke, VA 24020-1694
(703) 362-6301

Special Interest Summer Programs
Mary Baldwin College
Staunton, VA 24401
(703) 885-0811, Ext. 276

Summer Scholars
Washington and Lee University
Lexington, VA 24450
(703) 463-8723

University of Virginia Young Writer's Workshop
University of Virginia
School of Education
Ruffner Hall 122
Charlottesville, VA 22903
(804) 924-0766

Washington

Summer Camps for High School Students
Pacific Lutheran University
Tacoma, WA 98447
(206) 535-7453

Wisconsin

College Bound for Dyslexic Students
Ripon College
P.O. Box 248
Ripon, WI 54971

Summer Sessions
Summer Sessions Office
University of Wisconsin at Madison
433 North Murray Street
Madison, WI 53706
(608) 262-2116

Natural Resources Workshops [University of Wisconsin at
   Stevens Point]
Workshop Coordinator
Natural Resources Careers Workshops
7290 County MM
Amherst Junction, WI 54407
(715) 824-2428

World Affairs Seminar
University of Wisconsin at Whitewater
Whitewater, WI 53190
(414) 472-1131

Wyoming

Summer Session
Central Wyoming College
Riverton, WY 82501
(307) 856-9291

Youth Exchange Programs and Study Abroad

Spending a year, a summer, or a semester living and studying in a foreign city can have the obvious benefits—investigating another culture firsthand, learning to appreciate new customs and values, maybe even picking up a second language—but your child can do some career exploring through one of these programs, too, especially if he or she is interested in:

☐ International business   ☐ Architecture   ☐ Music
☐ Art history   ☐ History   ☐ Fashion
☐ Anthropology   ☐ Foreign language   ☐ Literature
☐ Archeology   ☐ Culinary arts

Many study abroad programs have an academic component, allowing students to attend school regularly, or take specialized trips for short courses.

But first, you and your child need to do some research and planning ahead to make your child's dreams of visiting faraway places come true.

Check with your child's high school. Many high schools have worked closely over the years with certain agencies and all the liaison arrangements are already in place. Or, it might be that a local civic group such as Rotary International runs a study-abroad or exchange program through your child's school. Ask your child's counselor or the principal.

Check with your child's college. Colleges and universities sometimes offer junior-year study-abroad programs. While living on approved campuses abroad, students take courses that fit their majors. An entire year's credit accompanies them back to their home institutions, with the result that they graduate on schedule. Often the cost of these junior year programs is calculated so that a year studying in another country is not much more expensive than a normal year of study.

It could be that the college your child is attending or will attend offers such a program. Check the college's catalog. Usually *study abroad* is listed as just that in the index. Your child should meet with an academic adviser to plan course work so that spending a year abroad will not affect progress toward graduation.

Looking at Other Programs

There are many excellent study-abroad programs offered by independent organizations, too. But taking advantage of them requires a little more detective work on your part since they will not be sponsored by your child's high school or a college. Here's what you and your child need to do.

Know the sponsor. International exchange and study-abroad programs are not regulated by the U.S. government. Consequently, some will be better than others. Any information you need to evaluate a program should be readily available from the organization itself. Read the information carefully. Find out whether your college or university will accept credit earned elsewhere. Ask for clarification of any vague statements or claims. Finally, request to talk with a previous participant to get advice and information.

Understand the costs. Know what the basic fee will cover (travel, accommodations, books, etc.), whether medical and accident insurance is included in the fee, and what will happen should your child have to cancel before completing the program.

Investigate housing and classroom facilities. What you might consider modest living arrangements would seem like luxury in another country. Find out in advance about the living arrangements, and about the adequacy of the instructional environment.

Compare the program's objectives with your own. Some study-abroad programs emphasize sightseeing, while others put the accent on academics. Find out what your child will accomplish while abroad and decide whether this fits in with the goals you've both established.

Review the course work and the staffing. If your child's objective is to study at a foreign university, he or she should find out: What will be taught and in what language will instruction be given? Who will be teaching and what are their credentials? Will there be an adviser or a director-in-residence who can help if necessary?

Study abroad can be a ticket to excitement, fun, and learning if you and your child do your homework about various programs first. An excellent guide is *Study and Teaching Opportunities Abroad,* a 68-page booklet prepared by Pat Kern McIntyre, formerly of the U.S. Office of Education. You can order a copy from the Government Printing Office, Washington, DC 20402.

Organizations Offering Exchange and Study-Abroad Programs

Organizations recommended by the Council on Standards for International Educational Travel are listed below.

Academic Travel Abroad, Inc.
3210 Grace Street NW
Washington, DC 20007
(202) 333-3355

Countries Served: China, Egypt, England, Finland, France, New Zealand, Spain, USSR

Adventures in Real Communications, Inc.
4162 Giles Road
Chagrin Falls, OH 44022
(216) 247-4214

Countries Served: Canada, Costa Rica, France, Germany, Mexico, Spain, USSR

AFS (American Friends Service) International/Intercultural Programs
313 East 43rd Street
New York, NY 10017
(212) 949-4242

Countries Served: Argentina, Australia, Austria, Barbados, Belgium, Bolivia, Brazil, Canada, Chile, China, Colombia, Costa Rica, Cyprus, Denmark, Dominican Republic, Ecuador, Egypt, Fiji, Finland, France, Germany, Ghana, Greece, Greenland, Honduras, Hong Kong, Hungary, Iceland, India, Indonesia, Ireland, Israel, Italy, Jamaica, Japan, Jordan, Kenya, Liberia, Luxembourg, Malaysia, Malta, Mexico, Morocco, Netherlands, New Zealand, Northern Mariana Islands, Norway, Panama, Paraguay, Peru, Portugal, Puerto Rico, Singapore, South Africa, South Korea, St. Lucia, St. Vincent and the Grenadines, Spain, Sri Lanka, Sweden, Switzerland, Thailand, Tunisia, Turkey, United Kingdom, Uruguay, USA, USSR, Venezuela, Yugoslavia

Alexander Muss High School in Israel
3950 Biscayne Boulevard
Miami, FL 33137
(305) 576-3286

Countries Served: Israel, USA

American Council for International Studies
19 Bay State Road
Boston, MA 02215
(617) 236-2051

Countries Served: Austria, Belgium, Canada, Czechoslovakia, Denmark, France, Germany, Great Britain, Greece, Mexico, Morocco, Netherlands, Spain, Switzerland, USA, USSR

The American Heritage Association
P.O. Box 425
Lake Oswego, OR 97034
(503) 635-3703

Countries Served: China, France, Germany, Great Britain, Greece, Hong Kong, Italy, Japan, Mexico, Spain, Switzerland, USA, Wales, Yugoslavia

American Institute for Foreign Study, Inc.
102 Greenwich Avenue
Greenwich, CT 06830
(203) 869-9090

Countries Served: Austria, Belgium, Bulgaria, China, Denmark, Egypt, England, France, Germany, Greece, Hong Kong, Hungary, Ireland, Israel, Italy, Japan, Kenya, Mexico, Netherlands, Poland, Scotland, Singapore, Spain, Switzerland, Taiwan, Thailand, Turkey, USA, Yugoslavia

American Institute for Foreign Study Scholarship Foundation
102 Greenwich Avenue
Greenwich, CT 06830
(203) 625-0755

Countries Served: Austria, Brazil, Colombia, Finland, Germany, Hong Kong, Japan, Malaysia, Netherlands, Saudi Arabia, Spain, Sweden, Switzerland, USA

American Intercultural Student Exchange
7728 Lookout Drive
La Jolla, CA 92037
(619) 459-9761

Countries Served: Austria, Australia, Belgium, Brazil, Colombia, Denmark, Ecuador, Finland, France, Germany, Ireland, Italy, Japan, Netherlands, Norway, Spain, Sweden, Switzerland, USA

American International Youth Student Exchange Program
200 Round Hill Road
Tiburon, CA 94920
(415) 435-4049

Countries Served: Australia, Austria, Belgium, Canada, Denmark, France, Great Britain, Greece, Ireland, Italy, Japan, Netherlands, Portugal, Spain, Sweden, Switzerland, West Germany

Amigos de las Americas
5618 Star Lane
Houston, TX 77057
(713) 782-5290
(800) 231-7796 or in Texas (800) 392-4580

Countries Served: Costa Rica, Dominican Republic, Ecuador, Mexico, Paraguay, Panama

ASSE International Student Exchange Programs
228 North Coast Highway
Laguna Beach, CA 92651
(714) 494-4100

Countries Served: Australia, Belgium, Canada, Denmark, England, Finland, France, Germany, Iceland, Netherlands, New Zealand, Northern Ireland, Norway, Scotland, Spain, Sweden, Switzerland, USA, Wales

AYUSA International
151 Union Street, Suite 506
San Francisco, CA 94111
(415) 434-1212

Countries Served: Denmark, England, Finland, France, Germany, Hong Kong, Japan, Malaysia, Mexico, Netherlands, Norway, Philippines, Spain, Sweden, Thailand, USA

Citizen Exchange Council
18 East 41st Street
New York, NY 10017
(212) 889-7960

Countries Served: China, Eastern Europe, USA, USSR

Educational Foundation for Foreign Study
1425 Chapala Street
Santa Barbara, CA 93101
(805) 963-0553

Countries Served: Austria, Belgium, Canada, Colombia, Denmark, Finland, France, Germany, Great Britain, Italy, Japan, Mexico, Netherlands, Norway, Philippines, Spain, Sweden, Switzerland, USA

Experiment in International Living
Kipling Road
Brattleboro, VT 05301
(802) 257-7751

Countries Served: Argentina, Australia, Belgium, Bolivia, Brazil, Cameroon, Canada, Chile, China, Colombia, Czechoslovakia, Denmark, Ecuador, England, France, Germany, Greece, Hong Kong, India, Indonesia, Iran, Ireland, Italy, Japan, Kenya, Korea, Malaysia, Mexico, Nepal, New Zealand, Nigeria, Norway, Panama, Paraguay, Philippines, Poland, Portugal, Saudi Arabia, Spain, Sweden, Switzerland, Taiwan, Thailand, Turkey, Venezuela

Iberoamerican Cultural Exchange Program
13920 93rd Avenue NE
Kirkland, WA 98034
(206) 821-1463

Countries Served: Costa Rica, Guatemala, Mexico, Spain, USA

International Christian Youth Exchange
134 West 26th Street
New York, NY 10001
(212) 206-7307

Countries Served: Australia, Austria, Belgium, Bolivia, Colombia, Costa Rica, Denmark, Finland, France, Germany, Ghana, Honduras, Iceland, India, Italy, Japan, Liberia, Mexico, New Zealand, Nicaragua, Nigeria, Norway, South Korea, Sweden, Switzerland, Turkey, USA

International Education Forum
P.O. Box 5107
San Ramon, CA 94583-0707
(415) 866-9696

Countries Served: Belgium, Brazil, Colombia, Czechoslovakia, Denmark, Finland, France, Germany, Italy, Japan, Mexico, Netherlands, Portugal, Spain, Sri Lanka, Sweden, Switzerland, Thailand

International Student Exchange, Inc.
P.O. Box 58
Fort Jones, CA 96032
(916) 468-2264

Countries Served: Belgium, Germany, Japan, Mexico, Spain, USA

International Travel Study, Inc.
4200 4th Street North, Suite 1
St. Petersburg, FL 33703
(813) 525-2096

Countries Served: Barbados, Brazil, Canada, Colombia, Costa Rica, Czechoslovakia, England, Finland, France, Germany, Greece, Hungary, Ireland, Japan, Martinique, Mexico, Netherlands, Spain, Switzerland, USA, Yugoslavia

Intropa International, USA
1066 Saratoga Avenue, Suite 100
San Jose, CA 95129
(408) 247-5574

Countries Served: Austria, China, Czechoslovakia, France, Germany, Great
Britain, Hungary, Italy, Japan, Switzerland, USA

National Registration Center for Study Abroad
823 North Second Street
P.O. Box 1393
Milwaukee, WI 53201
(414) 278-0631

Countries Served: Australia, Belgium, Costa Rica, Denmark, Dominican
Republic, England, France, Germany, Hong Kong, Italy, Japan, Luxembourg,
Mexico, Netherlands, New Zealand, Portugal, Scotland, Spain, Sweden,
Switzerland, USA

Open Door Student Exchange
250 Fulton Avenue
P.O. Box 71
Hempstead, NY 11551
(516) 486-7330

Countries Served: Argentina, Bolivia, Brazil, Canada, Chile, Colombia, Costa
Rica, Denmark, Ecuador, Egypt, El Salvador, England, France, Germany,
Guatemala, Honduras, Hong Kong, Israel, Italy, Jamaica, Japan, Mexico,
Peru, Spain, Sweden, Uruguay, USA, Yugoslavia

PEACE-USA
P.O. Box 29497
Columbus, OH 43229
(614) 848-5660

Countries Served: Hong Kong, Japan, USA

People to People High School Student Ambassador Program
110 Ferrall Street
Spokane, WA 99202
(509) 534-0430

Countries Served: Australia, Austria, Belgium, China, Czechoslovakia,
Denmark, East Germany, England, Fiji, Finland, France, Germany, Greece,
Hong Kong, Hungary, Ireland, Italy, Japan, Netherlands, New Zealand,
Norway, Portugal, Scotland, South Korea, Spain, Sweden, Switzerland,
Taiwan, USA, USSR, Yugoslavia

School Partnerships International (SPI)

National Association of Secondary School Principals
1904 Association Drive
Reston, VA 22091
(703) 860-0200

Countries Served: Austria, Canada, Costa Rica, France, Germany, Israel, Italy, Japan, Spain, United Kingdom, USA, Venezuela

Spanish Heritage-Herencia Española

116-53 Queens Boulevard
Forest Hills, NY 11375
(718) 268-7565

Countries Served: Mexico, Spain, USA

Student Travel Schools, Inc.

19 Charmer Court
Middletown, NJ 07748
(201) 671-6448

Countries Served: Denmark, Norway, Sweden

Up With People

3103 North Campbell Avenue
Tucson, AZ 85719
(602) 327-7351

Countries Served: Belgium, Canada, China, Denmark, England, Finland, France, Germany, Ireland, Italy, Japan, Liechtenstein, Luxembourg, Mexico, Netherlands, Norway, Portugal, Scotland, Spain, Sweden, Switzerland, USA

World Experience

2440 South Hacienda Boulevard, Suite 116
Hacienda Heights, CA 91745
(818) 330-5719

Countries Served: Australia, Bolivia, Brazil, Canada, Chile, Colombia, Denmark, Finland, France, Germany, Mexico, Norway, Panama, Spain, Sweden, USA

Youth for Understanding

3501 Newark Street NW
Washington, DC 20016
(202) 966-6800

Countries Served: Argentina, Australia, Belgium, Brazil, Chile, Colombia, Denmark, Ecuador, El Salvador, England, Finland, France, Germany, Greece, Ireland, Japan, Mexico, Netherlands, Norway, Paraguay, Philippines, Scotland, Spain, Sweden, Switzerland, USA, Uruguay, Venezuela, Wales

8

Getting the Most Out of A First Job

Do you remember your first job? Maybe it was something simple like raking leaves for your aunt, for which she paid you a quarter. Or maybe it was a traditional sort of first job like delivering newspapers, babysitting, or working in a concession stand. In any event, it was a significant experience in your life: most people can remember their first job as well as they can their first date.

A child's introduction to the world of work through a first job is important, not because it determines a career—first jobs are usually pretty mundane—but because it gives young people a chance to develop good work habits. Good habits not only stand them in good stead no matter how many occupations they sample during a lifetime, but also open doors to other, and usually better, opportunities. In other words, the more you help your child polish his or her work-style now, the bigger the payoff will be in the future.

Is there a trick for guaranteeing success at a first job? No, not really. It's a matter of being *prepared* to work: having a plan for finding the right job, demonstrating an attitude that will impress employers, and performing responsibly on the job. With these things in mind, your child can turn a first job into a big step toward the right career, and needn't depend on "lucky breaks" along the way.

Password? Maturity

Through my contacts with hundreds of employers over the years, I hear the same refrain about young workers: "Why can't they be more responsible?" By responsible, employers don't mean that young people aren't allowed to make mistakes occasionally—drop a crate of vegetables, mistotal a bill—but that there are *certain expectations related to maturity* that employers yearn to see demonstrated. For example:

Young workers will dress appropriately for work.

They'll be on time.

They won't call at the last minute and plead illness or some emergency.

They will be conscientious about their responsibilities.

They will cooperate with other employees.

They'll be honest.

These may not seem like impossible expectations, but it's failure to meet them that usually compels employers to fire their young workers, not stealing or inability to do the job.

In fact, something that will give your child an edge over other young people in finding a job, keeping a job, and moving on to a better job, is demonstrating maturity every step of the way.

Step 1: Go After the Right Job

The purpose of this book is to help your child define occupational interests. How good the fit is between your child and an occupation has a lot to do with whether he or she will enjoy the work and succeed at it.

Most young people, however, take the shotgun approach to working, especially with their first job. Rather than think where they would like to work, where they might have fun, they just look for a job—any job. The risk, of course, is that they'll land a real clinker, grouse about it, and eventually come to the conclusion that working is boring and unrewarding. So instead of their first job becoming a gala premiere, it ranks in their mind with what they've heard about boot camp.

In going after a first job, your child should pursue his or her interests: a job in a hobby shop, a lumber yard, a gas station, a boutique—any place with real appeal (refer back to Chapters 7 and 4 for ideas). Not only will this approach inspire job-hunting efforts, but your child's enthusiasm will probably be apparent to those doing the hiring. One girl I know of, for example, wanted to work in a bakery shop—it was an image of herself she liked. So she went to the only bakery shop in town every few weeks and inquired about a job. She left her name and phone number. As you can predict, it wasn't long before she was hired. Who else had shown such consistent interest?

Step 2: Identify Places to Apply

The Help Wanted ads are where most people turn to look for jobs, but in fact most employers don't advertise entry-level jobs. Here's how your child can generate job leads.

Networking. You and your child know neighbors, friends, and relatives. Have your child spend an hour on the phone calling them and saying, "If you know of a job that has to do with (be specific: helping people, selling products, repairing machines, for example), or you know of someone in the business, please let me know." Most adults will go to bat for a young person with this kind of ambition. Second, if your child participated in one of the shadowing experiences suggested in Chapter 7, valuable contact has already been made. Perhaps there are employment opportunities at that place of business. Or your child can ask her sponsor for names of contacts. Either way, shadowing is a sophisticated job-hunting technique that works.

The Yellow Pages. There are directories of professional associations for the more advanced job-seeker, and many of these organizations maintain job listings, but your child is probably not at this stage. The local Yellow Pages directory, on the other hand, lists all the businesses in your area. Use the headings on each page to target potential employers. A girl I counseled said she wanted to be around animals. Looking in the Yellow Pages, she was surprised to learn that there were five kennels and four pet stores in the area. Eventually, she was offered two jobs. Encourage your child to make a list of all the places she might apply. And remember, these places should be ones where she has a genuine interest in working.

Step 3: Get Outfitted for the Job Hunt

Your child can fill out countless job applications and still not land a job. Why? Because other youngsters are doing the same thing and employers have a stack of applications to choose from when a position

Sample Résumé

DENIS KERASOTES

13458 Austin Boulevard
Elkhart Lake, MO 53819
(312) 568-1304

EDUCATION

Rich East Township High School, September 1987–
  present
Blackhawk Junior High School, September 1985–June
  1987
Mohawk Elementary School, September 1979–June 1985

High school grade-point average: B

WORK EXPERIENCE

Rudy's Supermarket, bagger and stockboy, summer 1987
Elkhart Lake Park District recreational worker,
  summer 1986

VOLUNTEER

Boy Scouts, assistant troop leader, 1986–present
Little League assistant coach, 1986–1987

SCHOOL EXTRACURRICULAR ACTIVITIES

Member of photography club, 1987–present
Class treasurer, 1987

REFERENCES ON REQUEST

opens up. Also, written job applications deprive young people of the opportunity to really introduce themselves and make a lasting impression. The information requested—age, address, previous jobs held, etc.—is impersonal, not likely to make an employer think, "Hmm, here's one that's really different—let's give him a call." Actually, applications are used more often to screen people out than to draw attention to the best candidates.

Instead, I recommend to students that they arm themselves with the same equipment used by savvy adults: a résumé. And that they follow-up on contacts in ways I'll describe. These tactics go right around the first major obstacle, the job application, and demonstrate that essential difference, *maturity*, that employers are eager to find in young people. If your child objects that putting together a résumé sounds like too much trouble, point out that his competition is probably thinking exactly the same thing. Most students don't take the time to sell themselves the way an adult would. Consequently, most students don't get hired. Suggest that your child use the format of the résumé for Denis Kerasotes.

Step 4: Deliver the Résumé in Person

What should your child do with the résumé? Well, he could have 200 run off and mail them, along with a cover letter, to various places of business, but that takes time and it can be expensive. Also, he may not get a reply for some time, if at all. But since your child is mainly thinking about nearby places of business, it's simpler just to deliver the résumés in person. The big advantage to this technique is the impact it has on employers.

Salespeople call this making cold calls; here's how it works. Your child goes to selected possible workplaces, asks to see the manager, shakes hands, offers the résumé, and adds that he or she would be pleased to come in at the manager's convenience for an interview. It wouldn't be uncommon for the manager to say, "Why don't you just step into my office and we'll talk right now?" After all, who else is on file who appeared in person with a résumé? You guessed it: practically no one. That's why your son or daughter will get special attention.

Your son or daughter, of course, may not like this idea. Words like "silly, embarrassing, foolish" and others will be raised as objections. Your best response to what are normal adolescent fears is to be a good listener. Here's how the scenario might go:

Child: Mom, I can't do that—it's too embarrassing.

You: You're worried about being embarrassed.

Child: Sure, it would be awful.

You: Why? What might happen?

Child: Well, what if the manager's not in? Then what do I do?

You: What do you think would be a good idea?

Child: Just leave it for him, I guess.

You: What else might be embarrassing?

Child: I don't know . . . I'll just feel dumb introducing myself like that.

You: Why don't we practice a couple of times?

Child: Practice? C'mon.

You: I'll be the manager and you say . . . well, what do you think you should say?

Child: That I'm looking for a job—here's my résumé.

You: Okay, and what would be a good note to leave on?

Child: Call me if you have anything.

You: Right, let's try it.

Role-playing, in fact, may go a long way toward relieving your child's anxiety about the process. Try it and be complimentary. You might even try role-playing the next step: the interview.

Step 5: Plan a Successful Interview

Interviews go well when the job-seeker is prepared. This means being on time, dressing in a business-like manner, bringing a copy of the résumé along, and being prepared to answer questions. Sometimes interviews are immediate, particularly in connection with entry-level jobs. Other times, interviews are scheduled.

One of the keys to having a successful interview is thinking about answers to routine questions in advance. Here are some favorites among employers:

Why should we hire you?
Tell me a bit about yourself.

Why are you interested in working here?

Would you be available to work regularly and maybe even overtime, if necessary?

How well do you work under pressure?

What two or three of your accomplishments have given you the most satisfaction? Why?

And here are some DON'TS your child should keep in mind:

Don't go in not knowing very much about the business (places to learn about businesses include the local Chamber of Commerce, the state employment office, county and city offices, colleges in your community, union halls, youth centers, job counseling services offered by churches or civic organizations).

Don't bring a friend to the interview.

Don't avoid making eye contact. Hold the interviewer's gaze.

Don't fiddle with objects—pens, pencils, paper clips, etc.

Don't slouch. Sit up straight.

But suppose the manager wasn't in, or he doesn't have a job opening. What's your child's next move?

Step 6: Call Back

I tell students to call back in two weeks and say they're still interested. A week after that, call back again. The idea isn't to pester anyone, but just to make it clear that you are determined. Perseverance is a good sign in a potential employee.

Finally, the last step: it may not seem like it will add anything to a job campaign, but it can be very effective.

Step 7: Send a Thank-You Note

A thank-you note returns to the theme of maturity again. Most young people fill out an application, perhaps even have an interview, and then aren't heard from again. A simple courtesy like sending a thank-you note makes a terrific impression. If a job does open up, the first candidate who'll come to the employer's mind will be, "Let's see, who was that young person? The one who sent a thank-you note?" Let it be your child.

Ten Ways to Keep a Job

Once your child has a job, the next objective is to keep it. Some people think that saying "yes" to a job offer is crossing the finish line. But that's when the work begins and workers begin being evaluated. An employer making a job offer is saying, "We'll give you chance," not "You're safe here as long as you want to stay."

Have your child read the following ten ways to keep a job:

1. *Look right for the job.* Party clothes are not right for business. Sportswear *might* be right in some cases. The best advice is to either ask whether there is a dress code or to simply observe how other workers dress at the establishment and do likewise.

2. *Be on time, coming and going.* Peope who come in late, take long lunch hours, or leave early are cheating the boss of the time he or she is paying for. Don't think this won't be noticed—it will.

3. *If you can't come to work, let the boss know as early as possible.* No business can operate without workers. Your boss needs to know if you can't be there so that someone else can be brought in to do your work that day.

4. *Do the work that has to be done.* Every job has parts of it that aren't fun. Some secretaries hate to file; some mechanics hate to clean up and put away tools; but your work isn't finished until every segment of it is done.

5. *When you're on the job, work on the job.* Horsing around, talking too much with other workers, or making personal phone calls all take away from work. Business hours are for business.

6. *Be polite to everyone.* Get along with people. Keep your temper even if someone is rude to you. You'll notice that the best people to work with are the ones who are always willing to help. Be like those people.

7. *Do what you are asked to do.* You might be asked to do work that you didn't think you were hired to do. It happens to everyone. Don't argue about it, just do it as well as you can.

8. *Get to be good at your job.* Learn to do your job fast and well. When your employer needs someone for a better job, he or she will probably consider a current employee first. If you've done your job well, you'll be first in line for the promotion.

9. *Be able to take instruction.* You might think you know more than your boss, but proving that you're right by ignoring instructions is counter-productive. Listen to what you're told; make suggestions as tactfully as possible.

10. *Be able to take criticism.* Don't assume you're being picked on if your boss tells you you're doing something wrong. Concentrate on learning how to do the job correctly so there'll be no cause for criticism the next time.

Five Ways To Get the Most from a Job

Now let's move on to a more positive note—all of the "Ten Ways To Keep a Job" tended to be caveats. Here are five ways to get the most from a job, all of which are benefits your child can enjoy from working:

1. *Get training and learn new skills.* Résumés expand and job applicants can boast of more abilities as a result of what they have learned on previously held jobs. Young people should try to learn new skills— how to run machines, perform various operations, exercise responsibility—so that they can later point to these as evidence of their competence.

2. *Secure the job.* Students sometimes have to stop working because of other commitments such as extracurricular activities, grades, or going off to college. Your child should perform her work with the intent of securing a spot for herself so that she can always come back, if desired.

3. *Tackle personal challenges.* Your child might be shy. Working is an opportunity to overcome this trait. On the other hand, your child might need to experience success. In that case, working can provide the encouragement, too.

4. *Learn to cooperate.* Work involves people, and having or lacking "people skills" has a lot to do with success. Suggest that your child make a goal of learning to work harmoniously with others, and praise him when he describes the times he has done so.

5. *Get a strong recommendation.* Although references don't seem to be as influential as they once were, your child's employer can open new doors for her provided she's been an exemplary worker. Point out to your child that the employer has many contacts, contacts that

may act as a ladder carrying employees closer and closer to realizing their ambitions.

So far, we've been talking about your child working for someone else. But young people who are self-starters and can manage their own affairs in a mature way might want to consider independent work.

Becoming a Teenage Entrepreneur

Many students complain about the low-paying job rut: working at unskilled jobs where the pay is hardly worth salting away. One way to beat the system, according to Sarah Riehm, author of *The Teenage Entrepreneur's Guide—50 Money Making Business Ideas* (Surrey Books), is to start up an independent venture. "By running a small business rather than taking jobs," said Riehm, "teenagers eliminate a major obstacle they would otherwise face: they are free, within reason, to set their own wages and time schedule."

Being a young entrepreneur doesn't take a rich uncle, nor is it necessary to study the *Wall Street Journal.* All that's needed is a marketable idea, enthusiasm, and a *plan.* Here are the basic steps to success your son or daughter would need to follow.

1. *Find a product or service people will buy.* Proven entrepreneurial enterprises include:

    Teaching computer lessons

    Designing computer software

    Providing a garage sale service

    Washing or walking dogs

    Growing and selling vegetables

    Painting houses

    Videotaping weddings

    Photographing or videotaping valuables for insurance purposes

    Making and selling kites or other toys

    Washing windows

    Designing and silkscreening T-shirts

    Sharpening lawn mowers, scissors, knives, and skates

    Providing a cleaning service

    Repairing lawnmowers, motorcycles, or bikes

    Providing day care for children or elderly adults

    Catering parties

    Refinishing wood floors

    Tutoring younger children

2. *Think of a descriptive name.* Some student businesses have names that cleverly define the product or service they provide. "House About a Paint Job?" "Maid Day! Maid Day!" "I Do Windows" "Toys 'R Me" and "Mow, Mow, Mow Your Lawn" are some I've seen.

3. *Have the necessary equipment.* If the equipment is family-owned, the student should be sure to secure permission to use it, and should remember to schedule its use so as not to interfere with family needs. Buying used equipment or renting it are also possibilities.

4. *Do some effective advertising.* A pair of high school boys who wanted to paint houses ran flyers off and put them on car windshields in a supermarket parking lot. They generated so much business that they had to hire 4 helpers to finish 40 houses by September.

5. *Follow-through on commitments to clients.* Who knows? A summer business could become a lucrative, full-time occupation eventually.

Van Hutchinson, a 22-year-old who wrote *College Cash: How to Earn and Learn as a Student Entrepreneur* (Harcourt Brace Jovanovich), recommends that young people get as much informed help and advice as possible along the way. "Seek out positive, encouraging people—such as a relative or friend who has succeeded in business—who will believe in and guide you," he said. "The world is filled with narrow-minded people who can't imagine a young person succeeding. Leave these pessimists in the dust. Instead, imagine the possibilities."

Perhaps you could be that "positive, encouraging" person when your child starts his or her own business.

Good Jobs: No College Needed

An alternative we haven't talked about yet is working full-time either during the summer or after graduation from high school. It could be that your child is eager to get to work and to be self-supporting—additional education or training might come later. If so, your child may want to study the following list of good-paying jobs ($15,000 a year and more) that are suitable for young adults. In some cases, however, applicants have to be at least 18 years old because the job is considered hazardous. (See the list of occupations designated as hazardous by the Secretary of Labor on page 160.)

Occupation	Training/Education
Airline Radio Operator, Chief Coordinates activities of airline-radio operators in maintaining radio communications with aircraft and neighboring ground stations. Makes emergency repairs to equipment and examines new equipment prior to installation.	Must be high school graduate. Air communication training from a technical institute helpful.
Airplane Inspector Examines airframe, engines, and operating equipment of aircraft to insure that repairs are made according to specifications. Collects data to evaluate engine performance. Approves or rejects repairs.	Must be high school graduate. Most inspectors learn their jobs in the Armed Forces or in trade schools.
Avionics Technician Inspects, tests, adjusts, and repairs aircraft communication, navigation, and flight control systems. Tests and replaces defective equipment.	High school graduates preferred. Vocational or junior college training helpful.
Boat Loader Connects hose couplings to enable liquid cargo, such as petroleum, gasoline, heating oil, sulfuric acid, and alum liquor to be pumped from and into barges and tankers.	Must be 18. High school not required but preferred.
Bookkeeper Keeps income and expense ledgers for individuals or businesses.	High school graduate preferred with course work in basic accounting or bookkeeping.
Buyer Acquires merchandise for stores and wholesale outlets. Usually specializes in one type of product.	High school graduate preferred. Some education in business practices helpful.
Carpenter Builds and repairs structures and fixtures of wood, plywood, and wallboard to conform to building codes. Studies blueprints and prepares layout. Puts up framework for structures and builds stairs and walls. Installs prefabricated window frames, doors, and trim.	High school or vocational school education desirable. Apprenticeship recommended.

Occupation	Training/Education
Carpenter, Maintenance Constructs and repairs structural wood-work and equipment working from blue-prints, drawings, or oral instructions. Builds, installs, or repairs wood struc-tures.	High school or vocational school education preferred. Apprenticeship recom-mended.
Chemical Operator Works in plant where industrial chemical products are manufactured into finished products. Sets dials, valves, and other controls to insure that the correct temper-ature, pressure, and amounts of material are used.	High school graduate pre-ferred.
Coater Operator Operates machine which coats coils of sheet metal, flat metal blanks, or metal parts with paint, vinyl plastic, or adhesive film. Starts machine and regulates speed and temperature. Inspects coated metal for defects.	High school diploma not required.
Coil Winder Works in electronic manufacturing plants winding coils to be used in electrical equipment and instruments. Works ac-cording to diagrams and special instruc-tions.	High school diploma not re-quired. Aptitude test may be administered.
Composition Weatherboard Applier Applies composition weatherboard to outside of buildings using carpenter's handtools. Cuts, fits, and nails sections of weatherboard to building.	Employers in the building trades prefer high school graduates.
Computer Operator Runs programs on computers and moni-tors computer-controlled functions.	High school graduate pre-ferred. Course work in key-boarding helpful.
Die Maker Lays out, fits, and assembles castings and metal parts to make and repair stamping dies. Studies blueprints and specifications. Plans machining, layout, and assembly operations.	High school graduates pre-ferred. Technical schools and junior colleges offer courses which should be helpful.

Occupation	Training/Education
Diesel Engine Tester Analyzes performance of diesel engines and records temperatures of oil, water, and bearings. Replaces defective parts and adjusts engine.	High school or technical school graduate preferred.
Dispatcher, Motor Vehicle Assigns motor vehicles and drivers for conveyance or passengers. Handles customers' requests for pickup of freight and provides information on deliveries.	High school graduates preferred. Training is usually on the job.
Dragline Operator Operates power-driven crane equipped with dragline bucket, suspended from boom by cable to excavate or move sand, gravel, clay, mud, coal, or other materials.	High school graduate preferred.
Driller, Rotary Operates gasoline, diesel, electric, or steam draw works to drill oil or gas wells.	High school diploma helpful.
Drop Hammer Operator Sets up and operates closed-die drop hammer to forge metal parts following work order specifications.	High school diploma required.
Dry Wall Applicator Installs plasterboard or other wallboard to ceiling and inside walls of buildings. Nails wallboard to wall and ceiling supports.	High school diploma preferred but not required.
Electrician Installs and repairs wiring, electrical fixtures, and control equipment	High school or vocational school graduates preferred. Apprenticeship preferred.
Elevator Constructor Assembles and installs freight and passenger elevators and escalators.	High school or vocational school graduate preferred.
Engineer, Stationary Operates and maintains stationary engines and mechanical equipment such as steam engines, generators, motors, air compressors, turbines, and steam boilers to provide light, heat, and power for buildings and industrial plants.	High school or trade school graduates preferred. Apprenticeship recommended.

Occupation	Training/Education
Floor Layer Shapes heated metal into forgings on power hammer or press equipped with open dies. Checks forging against specifications using rule and calipers.	High school diploma preferred but not required.
Interior Designer Provides suggestions for decorating home and business environments. Plans layouts and selects materials to be used in the overall scheme.	Success usually depends on referrals from former clients. Some post-high school training would be helpful.
Installer-Repairer, Line Installs and repairs telephone and telegraph lines, poles, and equipment. Digs holes and sets in telephone poles. Strings lines from pole to pole and from pole to building.	High school graduates preferred.
Laser Beam Color Scanner Operator Sets up and operates computer controlled laser beam color scanner to enlarge and screen film separations used in preparation of lithographic printing plates. Activates scanner and develops exposed film.	A high school diploma is usually required.
Layout Worker Lays out reference points and marks finished size on sheets, plates, tubes, and structural shapes for making, welding, and assembling structural metal products.	High school or vocational school graduates preferred.
Machinist, Automotive Sets up and operates metalworking machines, such as lathes and boring machines, to repair automotive engine parts.	High school or technical school graduation preferred.
Maintenance Repairer, Building Repairs and maintains commercial, industrial, and residential buildings such as factories, office buildings, and apartment houses. Paints structures and repairs woodwork.	High school diploma preferred. Vocational education classes helpful.

Occupation	Training/Education
Mechanic, Aircraft Installs heating, plumbing, and hydraulic systems in aircraft according to blueprints. Tests installed units.	High school diploma recommended. Vocational education courses helpful.
Mechanic, Automobile Services, repairs, and overhauls automobiles, buses, trucks, and other automotive vehicles.	High school diploma preferred. Training can be on the job; vocational/technical school courses helpful.
Mechanic, Diesel Repairs and services diesel engines for buses, ships, railroad trains, trucks, electric generators, and construction machinery.	High school or vocational school graduate preferred.
Mechanic, Maintenance Repairs and services machinery and mechanical equipment such as production machines and conveyor systems. Takes devices apart and repairs or replaces defective parts. Lubricates and cleans parts.	High school graduate preferred. Vocational/technical school courses helpful.
Model Models garments such as dresses, coats, swimwear, and suits for garment designers, sales personnel, and customers. It is possible to freelance as a model.	Employers prefer high school graduates; some prefer applicants with college classes, too.
Natural Gas Treatment Unit Operator Operates automatically controlled natural gas treating unit in oilfield. Opens valves to admit gas and chemicals into treating vessels. Adjusts heat and pressure levels.	High school or trade school graduates preferred.
Painter, Sign Designs and paints signs. Reads work order to determine type of sign required. It is possible to freelance as a sign painter.	Training is available on the job or through apprenticeship.
Payroll Clerk Keeps records for businesses of sums paid to employees.	High school graduate preferred with course work in bookkeeping.

Occupation	**Training/Education**
Photojournalist Photographs scenes, incidents, or people as assigned by editor. Spends most of the workday going from one location to another.	Talent is the major requirement for this occupation. Many photojournalists begin their careers by freelancing.
Pipe Fitter Installs piping systems for steam, hot water, heating, cooling, sprinkling, lubrication, and industrial processing systems. Joins piping by cementing, caulking, welding, or other method.	High school or trade school graduates preferred. On the job and apprenticeship training available.
Plumber Installs and repairs pipes, fittings, and fixtures of heating, water, and drainage systems according to specifications and plumbing codes. Studies building plans; cuts openings in walls and floors.	High school or vocational school graduate preferred. On the job and apprenticeship training available.
Power Reactor Operator Controls nuclear reactor that produces steam for generation of electric power. Starts and shuts down reactor.	High school graduation required. Must be licensed by Nuclear Regulatory Agency.
Projectionist, Motion Picture Sets up and operates motion picture projection and sound-reproducing equipment. Monitors operation of machine. Repairs faulty sections of film. Some projectionists become theater managers.	High school graduates are generally preferred.
Refinery Operator Controls continuous operation of petroleum refining and processing units to produce products such as gasoline, kerosene, and fuel and lubricating oils. Reads schedules; tests results.	High school graduation usually preferred; most skills learned on the job.
Reservations Agent Assigns seating to passengers on commercial aircraft, checks their baggage, and assists them in locating their departure gate.	Must be a high school graduate.
Sales Representative for Radio and TV Time Sells air-time to businesses and individuals wanting to advertise their services. Most of the work is done by phone.	High school graduate preferred.

Occupation	Training/Education
Soft Tile Setter Applies decorative steel, aluminum, and plastic tile to walls and cabinets of bathrooms and kitchens.	Contractors usually prefer high school graduates.
Structural Steel Worker Works as member of crew to raise, place, and join girders, columns, and other structural-steel parts on buildings. Guides steel part into position; lines up rivet holes.	Apprenticeship program is recommended route. Training also available through the military.
Tool-and-Die Maker Makes and repairs metal-working dies, tools, and machine parts. Cuts and shapes parts using machine tools such as lathe, milling machine, shaper, and grinder. Joins parts using welding and brazing equipment.	High school or trade school diploma required. Apprenticeship recommended.
Travel Guide Accompanies groups or individuals on tours of places of interest, pointing out noteworthy sites and their characteristics.	High school graduate preferred. Courses in speech, theater, and history would be helpful.
Truck Driver Hauls shipments of all kinds on local, regional, or national routes.	Need not be a high school graduate. Truck driving school recommended.

Labor Laws Concerning Minors

The Federal government regulates the kind of occupations in which minors can be employed and what they shall be paid. Here's a summary of major provisions of the Fair Labor Standards Act.

Minimum Wage

The current minimum wage established by Federal law is $3.35 per hour. However, learners and minors may be paid at a lower rate. Learners may be paid $2.86 during the first 160 hours of employment.

Minors may also be paid at the $2.86-per-hour rate providing the number of minors being paid at the lower rate does not exceed 25 percent of the total number of employees. This 25 percent limitation does not apply during school vacations.

Hours of Employment and Permitted Occupations

Young people 18 years old or older may work 8 hours a day up to 40 hours a week. Overtime should be paid at the rate of 1½ times the normal rate if they work more than 8 hours a day. If they work over 12 hours a day, they are entitled to overtime at twice the hourly rate. Persons 18 years old and older may work in any occupation.

Teenagers who are 16 or 17 years old are not allowed to work more than 6 days a week. They may not be employed before 5 a.m. or after 10 p.m. unless there is no school the next day, but may work until 12:30 p.m. on a night that is not a school night. Young people in this age group may work in any occupation unless it is cited as hazardous by the Secretary of Labor (see below).

Children 14 or 15 years old may not work more than 8 hours a day on non-school days, or more than 3 hours a day on school days. They may not start work before 7 a.m. or work beyond 7 p.m. during the school year. From June 1 to Labor Day, regulations are relaxed and they may work 40 hours a week and until 9 p.m. Fourteen or 15 year olds may be employed in:

- Office and clerical work
- Cashiering, modeling, art work, work in advertising departments, window trimming, and comparative shopping
- Price marking and tagging by hand or machine
- Bagging and carrying out customers' orders
- Errand and delivery work by foot, bicycle, and public transportation
- Cleanup work including the use of vacuum cleaners and floor waxers; also, groundskeeping, but use of power-driven mowers and cutters is prohibited
- Kitchen work and other work involved in preparing and serving food including the operation of blenders, dishwashers, and toasters
- Work dispensing gas or oil, car cleaning or washing; however, use of pits, racks, or lifting apparatuses is prohibited
- Cleaning vegetables and fruits, and wrapping, sealing, labeling, weighing, pricing, and stocking goods; however, children this age are not permitted in areas where meat is prepared or in a meat freezer or cooler

Hazardous Occupations. Minors are not allowed to work in the following occupations unless they are part of a well-supervised school program:

- Manufacturing or storing explosives
- Driving motor vehicles and being an outside helper
- Coal mining
- Logging and sawmilling
- Operating power-driven woodworking machines
- Operating power-driven hoisting apparatuses
- Operating power-driven metal-forming, punching, processing, or rendering machines
- Operating power-driven bakery machines
- Manufacturing brick, tile, and kindred products
- Operating power-driven circular saws, band saws, and guillotine shears
- Wrecking, demolition, and ship-breaking operations
- Roofing operations
- Excavation operations

Exceptions to Child Labor Laws

Child labor law provisions do not apply to:

- Children under 16 years old employed by their parents in occupations other than manufacturing or mining or the hazardous occupations listed by the Secretary of Labor
- Children employed as actors or performers in motion pictures, theatrical, radio, or television productions
- Children engaged in the delivery of newspapers to the consumer
- Homemakers engaged in the making of wreaths or harvesting greens

More information about children being employed is available from the Wage and Hour Division of the U.S. Department of Labor. Look under the "U.S. Government" listing in your telephone book. If you have questions about state laws, call your state Department of Industrial Relations.

9

Opportunities
For Self-Knowledge
Through Additional
Education

As a result of reading this book, combined with the career exploration you've done on your own, you and your child may have decided that additional education beyond high school will be needed to realize career goals. But how *much* education? And what are the options?

There's a tendency among most people to think in terms of "college jobs" and "non–college jobs." In other words, ones that require a four-year degree and ones that don't. Actually, it would be more accurate to think in terms of a *spectrum* of educational opportunities available to your child, ranging from ones that require only a very short period of study to ones that require four or more years of higher education. If you're skeptical that without a four-year college degree only a handful of career choices will be available, here's a fact worth remembering: *over 60 percent of occupations require two years of college study or less.* That's right—a host of jobs in sales, health care, and technical work, for example, don't require bachelor's degrees. So if your child is drawn toward a future like this and shies away from the thought of going to college for four years, be confident that he or she is still on the right track.

On the other hand, your child may not have a firm idea of which career direction to move in. In that case, thinking in terms of a spectrum of post–high school study is again best. After all, if your child is uncertain about career choices, presenting only two alternatives—going to college or not going to college—might add to his or her indecision: what if I take the wrong road?

A third possibility is that your child is undecided about a career but has always included some kind of post–high school training or education in his or her plans. The reasons may be one or more of the following:

Because I want to get a good job

Because I want to learn how to get along with different kinds of people

Because I want to make contacts that will be important to me later in life

Because I want to learn how to figure out problems and know more about the world

These are all worthwhile educational goals that deserve praise. A concrete goal such as "I want to be a lawyer" is praiseworthy too, of course, but the main thing is the desire for additional self-knowledge through new educational challenges. Encourage this kind of thinking!

Let's look now at the spectrum of educational opportunities I've been talking about.

Correspondence Courses: The "Write Way" to Career Preparation

Imagine your child being able to receive instruction at home in a career field that he or she would like to sample: computer science, accounting, nutrition, bookkeeping—any one of over 12,000 courses. It's possible and inexpensive through correspondence study offered by 73 accredited colleges, universities, and home study organizations. In many cases, your son or daughter can receive college credit for passing the course.

To summarize the advantages of correspondence study, your son or daughter can:

Avoid scheduling and registration problems

Choose from a variety of well-known colleges and universities nationwide

Be exempt from the school's admission requirements
Explore new career areas
Save money

Correspondence study is demanding, however. Your child will need reasonably good reading and study skills. Moreover, since the work is done at the student's own pace, there are no deadline pressures to motivate finishing. It's unfortunate but true that many people don't complete correspondence courses. But with some supervision from you, your child can practice self-discipline and eventually know the thrill of having accomplished something important.

Most institutions offering undergraduate correspondence courses require no evidence of previous educational experience and no test scores from registrants. Only at the graduate level are prerequisites required, but in any case, check with the institution before your child enrolls. The office of correspondence study will be listed in the index of a college's catalog.

Once your child registers for a course and the fee is paid, your child will receive:

Study materials: a list of required textbooks and a syllabus of required readings

Textbooks: these may be sent directly from the institution or your child will be informed about where they can be purchased

Study assignments: a guide that divides the course into segments and assignments (many schools have rules concerning how quickly assignments can be turned in; beware of "speedy" courses)

Examinations usually must be administered by a proctor. Students can generally arrange for a test to be supervised at a nearby school or college.

Generally, correspondence courses are a lot less expensive than regular attendance at a college or university, but a few hidden costs may not be apparent. For example, textbooks are not included in the price of a course, and students must bear the costs of postage themselves. Also, some course materials—kits, audiovisuals, lab specimens—may be expensive. However, students can usually pay a security deposit that is partially refunded when the materials are returned.

Financial aid for correspondence study is not as available as it is for traditional college studies. But here are a few leads you may want to pursue:

Employers will sometimes pay for college course work; check with the personnel department.

Unions also have contracts with employers providing educational benefits for workers.

Veterans' and military benefits: veterans' assistance acts all have provisions for correspondence study, usually termed "independent study."

Vocational rehabilitation: nearly all states provide financial assistance to handicapped persons seeking an education; direct your questions to your state's department of vocational rehabilitation.

Institutional aid: many colleges and universities have a limited amount of financial aid available to persons enrolling in correspondence courses; contact the financial aid office.

Eventually, your child may want to have his or her correspondence credit transferred to another school or program. *Records and transcripts* with grades received for credit courses are maintained by the college or university offering correspondence study. To have credit transferred, your son or daughter must follow the normal procedure of requesting a transcript to be sent to another institution: call the registrar's office or send a letter (usually there's a small fee for the service). If possible, it's a good idea to check in advance whether an institution will accept correspondence study credit. A second consideration is that many institutions have a limit on the number of correspondence credits they will accept.

One other caveat to keep in mind is this: only enroll in correspondence courses at institutions accredited by the National University Continuing Education Association (NUCEA) (see chart on page 165). There are plenty of diploma mills out there—check credentials first.

Trade and Technical Schools

Each year, more than 100,000 people graduate from institutions accredited by the National Association of Trade and Technical Schools (NATTS). These are schools that have been judged by the association to offer comprehensive programs under the guidance of skilled teachers.

Trade and technical schools offer training to make a person job-ready for a specific occupation. Most of these schools are private, consequently their tuitions are higher than public community colleges, which offer many of the same programs. Nevertheless, some students

Accredited Institutions Offering Correspondence Study

Adams State College
Arizona State University
Arkansas State University
Auburn University
Brigham Young University
California State University at
  Sacramento
Central Michigan University
Colorado State University
Eastern Kentucky University
Eastern Michigan University
East Tennessee State University
Home Study Institute
Indiana State University
Indiana University
Louisiana State University
Loyola University of Chicago
Massachusetts Department of
  Education
Memorial University of
  Newfoundland
Mississippi State University
Murray State University
Northern Michigan University
Ohio University
Oklahoma State University
Oregon State University
Oregon State System of Higher
  Education
Pennsylvania State University
Purdue University
Roosevelt University
Savannah State College
Southern Illinois University at
  Carbondale
Texas Tech University
University of Alabama
University of Alaska
University of Arizona

University of Arkansas
University of California
University of Colorado
University of Florida
University of Georgia
University of Idaho
University of Illinois
University of Iowa
University of Kansas
University of Kentucky
University of Michigan
University of Minnesota
University of Mississippi
University of Missouri
University of Nebraska—Lincoln
University of Nevada at Reno
University of New Mexico
University of North Carolina
University of North Dakota
University of Northern Colorado
University of Northern Iowa
University of Oklahoma
University of South Carolina
University of South Dakota
University of Southern
  Mississippi
University of Tennessee
University of Texas at Austin
University of Utah
University of Washington
University of Wisconsin,
  Extension
University of Wyoming
Upper Iowa University
Utah State University
Washington State University
Western Illinois University
Western Michigan University
Western Washington University

Source: *Independent Study Catalog: NUCEA's Guide to Independent Study Through Correspondence Instruction, 1986–88*. New Jersey: Peterson's Guides, 1986.

prefer the suit-and-tie atmosphere of a vocational school. Also, most accredited trade and technical schools participate in the same federal and state financial aid programs as two-year colleges, making it possible for students to consider them as alternatives.

Finding out whether a trade or technical school is accredited by a national association is just the first question your child should ask *before* registering at any private job-training school. The other questions are:

What kinds of people will I find in classes with me?
What will be the *total* cost of my education, including books, fees, materials, and anything else?
What's the length of the course I'm interested in?
If I don't finish the course, will I still owe the balance of the cost?
Does the school offer financial aid?
Can I be put in touch with a student who has graduated from here?
Does the school offer a job placement service?
What percentage of graduates find jobs in their field?
How much can a graduate expect to make in the occupation that interests me?

In addition, you and your child should arrange to be taken on a tour of the school.

On pages 167 and 168 is a list of jobs requiring three years or less of postsecondary vocational training. Look under "Schools" in the Yellow Pages for trade and technical schools offering instruction in these fields. Your child's high school counselor may have some background information on trade and technical schools your child is looking into. For additional information about jobs that take two years or less to learn, write:

National Association of Trade and Technical Schools
2251 Wisconsin Avenue NW
Washington, DC 20007

Skills Training at Trade and Technical Schools

Occupation	Program Length (in weeks)
Acting	30–150*
Advertising Art	52–136*
Air Conditioning	12–73
Airline Personnel Training	11–34
Appliance Repair	12–72
Architectural Engineering	60–100
Art	16–92
Automotive Mechanics	14–50
Aviation Mechanics	33–84
Barber/Hair Stylist	32–53
Blueprint Reading	3–40
Brickmasonry	102
Broadcasting	10–92
Building Maintenance	52–60
Camera Service and Repair	16–50
Camp Instructor	12
Carpentry	102
Coin-operated Machine Repair	26
Computer Technician	15–62
Construction Technology	32–104
Culinary Arts	13–72
Dance Instructor	64
Data Processing	21–100
Dental Assistant	21–50
Dental Laboratory Technician	26–72
Diesel Mechanics	10–38
Dietetics	13–52
Diving	25
Dog Grooming	4–8
Drafting	17–88
Dressmaking and Design	3–88
Electricity	21–104
Electronics	24–108*
Emergency Medical Technician	9–34
Engraving	12
Estimating, Building	10
Fashion Design	34–99
Fashion Illustration	52–136*
Fashion Merchandising	5–74
Gunsmithing	69
Heating	12–24
Heavy Equipment Operator	3–10

* Course work may take longer than two years depending on the curriculum chosen.

Skills Training at Trade and Technical Schools (cont.)

Occupation	Program Length (in weeks)
Horsemanship	11–38
Hotel-Motel Training	15–16
Industrial Management	72
Inhalation Therapy Technician	37–52
Instrumentation	78–80
Interior Design	64–108*
Jewelry Design	12–40
Loss Prevention Security	16
Machine Shop	14–102
Meat Cutting	8
Mechanical Engineering Technology	64–108*
Medical Assistant	20–43
Medical Secretary	12–43
Medical Technician	48–72
Metallurgical Technology	77
Millinery	5–48
Motion Pictures	12–150*
Nurse's Aide	10–49
Office Machine Repair	15–50
Operating Room Technician	36–50
Optometric Assistant	16–60
Orthopedic Assistant	16
Painting and Decorating	102
Paperhanging	11
PBX Switchboard	12
Photography	12–150*
Pilot, Commercial	12–69
Plumbing	26
Printing	24–72
Real Estate Brokerage	6
Surveying	72
Tailoring	5–60
Tool and Die Making	28–108*
Travel Agent	12–34
Truck Driving	1–8
Upholstery	10–50
Veterinarian Assistant	28
Vocational Nursing	49
Watchmaking and Repairing	52
Welding	2–72
X-ray Technician	100

* Course work may take longer than two years depending on the curriculum chosen.

Opportunities Through Two-Year Colleges

There are approximately 1,200 two-year colleges in the United States, of which 85 percent are public community schools. Public two-year colleges were established to meet the needs of a diverse student population and to help these students decide on their educational and career goals. In many states, public two-year colleges are required to accept all high school graduates who are residents of the state or of the school district.

Community colleges offer low tuition, substantial career preparation, the chance to combine part-time work with schooling, and the opportunity to "test the waters" of college while still living at home. But the real selling point of the public two-year college system is its versatility: it offers three kinds of education.

Certificate programs. Much of the same kind of training available through trade and technical schools is offered by two-year colleges under the heading "certificate programs." Certificates, not degrees, are awarded for completed work in such fields as air-conditioning apprenticeship, teacher's aide, word processing, and tool-and-die maker apprenticeship. Some certificate programs are as short as two or three months, and some span a year or more. See the chart of occupations in the preceding section for an idea of the type of certificate programs offered through two-year colleges.

Two-year associate degrees. A two-year associate degree is a two-year college degree that is not transferable to a four-year institution. These "terminal" degrees are available in nursing, police science, real estate, secretarial science, dental hygiene, and many other areas.

Transfer degrees. Another kind of associate degree program educates students as though they were freshmen and sophomores in a four-year system. After graduating with a two-year associate degree in liberal arts, business, English, mathematics, or journalism, for example, students can transfer to a four-year institution and receive a bachelor's degree after two additional years of study. Understand, however, that if your child goes the community college route with the intention of transferring to a four-year school, he or she must take a *university parallel curriculum*. This means that freshman and sophomore courses must satisfy the requirements of the college he or she plans to attend.

This isn't hard to accomplish, but many transfer students lose a semester needlessly by neglecting to do a little research in advance. Your child should study the catalog of the four-year college carefully and talk with an admission counselor there to make sure of taking courses that will transfer. (See the following page for tips on transferring credit.)

Often two-year college students planning to transfer look back to their high school record as an indication of the type of four-year college they should consider. But it's the work completed in the two-year college that counts more. I encourage students not to underestimate themselves: pulling A's and B's at a two-year college is a sign to think about stepping up to competitive universities and four-year colleges.

"Here's what goes through the mind of a two-year college student," says Rob Yacubian, Coordinator of Transfers at Greenfield Community College in Greenfield, Massachusetts. "He thinks, 'I'll apply to a four-year public college—that's all I can handle.' But when that student comes to see me in that frame of mind, the first thing I do is catch him off guard with, 'Have you thought about a more competitive school?' "

Yacubian's job is to encourage transfer students to think about possibilities. Too often, he finds, they want to "move over" to a four-year college that's on exactly the same level. "They underestimate themselves, yes. But what they don't realize is that very often four-year colleges don't even look at high school grades. Community college grades count more. What admissions people realize about community college students is that maybe they weren't as mature in high school. Or maybe they just were not encouraged to do well in class. But that was then, this is now."

In her role as an admission representative for the University of Pennsylvania, Kelly Higashi has read many applications from community college transfer students. "We don't weigh the high school transcript as heavily as the one from the community college," she said. "We look at that first and foremost. It eclipses even the scores from the SAT or ACT taken in high school. The interview is very important, too."

Higashi says one of the key considerations is whether the transfer applicant has taken challenging courses at the community college. "They don't need to retake the SAT or ACT," she said. "We just want to see the kinds of courses taken and the grades received. Usually the cut-off is a 3.0 or B average."

"So the first thing to do," said Yacubian, "is to sit down with an adviser and look at completed course work. Whether a student has taken mainly liberal arts courses or mainly career courses makes a difference. Career majors don't always develop the kind of classroom skills that will be needed in a four-year college. If that's the case with a student, he might want to backtrack for a semester to pick up a few more liberal arts courses." Next, he said, it's important to get "strong, intelligent recommendations from instructors who know you and the work you do. These can be very influential." Finally, he tells students, "Don't talk money—it shouldn't even be an issue. Many highly selective schools have big endowments, a portion of which they put into financial aid. Get accepted first."

Overall, Yacubian said, the competitive four-year college will want to know:

What has the applicant done after high school?

What has he or she done in liberal arts courses?

What kind of recommendations can he or she supply?

What can this student contribute to the institution?

"Very often," said Higashi, "the transfer student is a late bloomer. But he or she can definitely change the whole academic picture from high school to a four-year college."

"But," Yacubian cautions, "competitive schools continue to be competitive once you're admitted. So if you don't want to work, don't consider competitive schools."

Transferring tips. Transferring is as important a transition as going from high school to college. Here are some tips on academic and social success that your youngster may find helpful:

1. At the two-year college level, enroll in basic courses such as freshman English, biology, and other courses generally recognized as part of the education of any freshman or sophomore college student. Steer away from chancy electives—Urban Renewal I, or Third World Challenges—that may not be recognized as transferable to any other institution.

2. Become thoroughly familiar with the transfer requirements of the four-year college you want to attend. This can be accomplished by making an appointment with an admission adviser there, taking along a copy of your transcript or test report and a course catalog from your previous school. The course catalog becomes important in case your new school wants to know what was taught in a specific course.

3. Realize that you may not be able to "take it all with you" no matter

where you go. But most degree programs are flexible enough to allow a considerable number of credits to count as electives. All that will happen is that the number of electives you can take at your new school will be reduced.

4. Be prepared for the accelerated pace should you transfer to a larger or more competitive institution. The experiences of University of Illinois senior Pat Rogge are typical of many transfer students:

> The paperwork of transferring wasn't hard at all, but I would recommend to anyone getting ready to transfer to ask about placement tests at the four-year college. Placement tests tell you which classes you belong in.
>
> Two of my biggest surprises, though, going from a small community college to a large university, was first, the enormous size of the university and second, how much the professors expect. When I walked into my first class, it was a lecture hall with maybe 200 people in it. The material was harder, the class moved faster, and they advised that you did not miss class. What you have to do is spot someone in class you think you could be friends with, and then help each other. That way if the class is tough, you can call someone and the two of you can work it out. Another thing you should do is skim ahead in the book—keep a little ahead of your work.
>
> I'd also recommend that transfer students take advantage of the counseling services. I did, and my counselor set me up with a tutor and gave me a few career interest tests that have been helpful.
>
> I guess that my overall advice is: prepare yourself—you're in for some changes.

5. Make an effort at meeting people and joining in. It's not necessary to go around at college acting like you're running for office and gladhanding everyone. There are simple ways to get into the swing of things and feel a part of campus life:

   - Keep your dormitory door open. Get to know the people on your floor.
   - Read the campus newspaper every day. Look for upcoming events and meetings that interest you and go to them.
   - Take advantage of freshman dances and mixers. Everyone there will be new and looking forward to meeting people.
   - Spend time at the student center where there are bulletin boards, game rooms, and lounges for just relaxing and talking.

- Don't wait until you're feeling left out to talk to someone about it. Drop in on your dorm's resident adviser or make an appointment to see a counselor at the student counseling center.

It's normal to feel some trepidation about meeting new people and having new experiences. The best thing you can do is jump in with both feet at every opportunity and participate.

6. Hit the books regularly and become a good time manager:

- *Locate a good study area.* It might be a cubicle in the library, or a room in the dormitory set aside for studying, but in any case it should be quiet and free from distractions.
- *Make a study schedule and stick to it.* Make a chart showing what you must do every day (attend class, go to work, etc.) and block out the in-between times for studying.
- *Make good use of peak times.* Some people study best early in the morning and some later in the day. But few can study well when they're tired. Avoid relying on the middle of the night as study time.
- *Use the SQ3R method of studying.* First, *survey* the assignment: read the title, the subheads, and the summary at the end. Turn key ideas or subheads into written *questions* as you go. Then begin to *read.* Stop at the end of each section and *recite* the information to yourself as though you were explaining it to a friend. Finally, *review* the assignment by glancing back at the main ideas and your questions.
- *Don't overstudy.* It's not necessary to hit the books all the time. Stick to your study schedule, then take a break from it and enjoy yourself. Maintaining a good attitude toward your work is important.

Going Directly to a Four-Year College or University

There are a number of first-rate guides worth reading on the subject of going directly from high school to a four-year college or university:

Gelband, Scott, Catherine Kubale, and Eric Schorr. *Your College Application.* New York: College Entrance Examination Board, 1986.

McGinty, Sarah Myers. *Writing Your College Application Essay.* New York: College Entrance Examination Board, 1986.

Ripple, Gary G. *Admit One! Your Guide to College Application.* Alexandria, VA: Octameron Associates, 1987.

Schneider, Zola Dincin. *Campus Visits and College Interviews.* New York: College Entrance Examination Board, 1987.

Generally, a college is an institution of higher learning that grants a bachelor's degree after four years of study. At most colleges, students can earn either a Bachelor of Science degree (B.S.) or a Bachelor of Arts (B.A.).

A *bachelor of arts degree (B.A.)* offers a cultural education through four years of study covering the arts, humanities, and social sciences. Students begin to concentrate during their third year on what they have selected as their major field of study: political science, literature, or biology, for example. A *bachelor of science degree (B.S.)* puts less emphasis on a broad liberal arts education, offering instead more preparation for a specific career in education, engineering, music, art, business, and other fields.

A university, on the other hand, encompasses a liberal arts college, plus separate undergraduate programs such as engineering or business, and various graduate programs that grant Master's degrees (M.A.) or Doctor of Philosophy degrees (Ph.D.). Universities also usually include graduate professional schools in such fields as law, architecture, and medicine.

Students often come to me trying to decide what they should major in that would match their career interests. I caution them that they'll have plenty of time to think about their major: freshmen and sopho-mores are required to take basic courses to give them a good foundation in liberal arts, regardless of their major. Not until junior year do they need to declare a major field of study.

But there are so many majors to choose from: how should your child go about choosing the right one? As I've tried to make clear in this book, the best advice about exploring careers (and this applies to choosing a major, too) is to find a good fit between the requirements of the vocation and the individual's interests and abilities. Unfortu-nately, some students don't ever really select a major—majors seem to select them. What happens is that these undergraduates find they've been taking a number of related courses in one area, and so they eventually declare this group as their major. This is the "instinct" approach to choosing a major, and it works for some students, although they don't exercise much self-direction this way. Who knows? Maybe if they had had a plan, a strategy, they would have had more *reasons* for selecting the major they did.

I recommend the following five-step plan to students for choosing a major:

Step 1: Experiment

As a way of making an informed choice about a major, take courses in college that you're curious about, not just ones that reinforce what you already know about yourself. Expand your information base, flex your mental muscles—experiment.

Step 2: Evaluate

It's not possible to do a thorough job of selecting a major without also doing some self-evaluation. This means taking an inventory of your interests and abilities so that your prospective major will make a good "fit." When it comes to linking your interests to your education, what's really at issue is what you want to do for a career. What will you enjoy learning that will prepare you for work?

If you're uncertain about your career interests, visit your high school counselor or adviser and ask to take a career interest survey. Colleges and universities maintain placement offices where students can take career interest surveys, research careers, receive counseling, and make appointments to see recruiters.

Next, look at your abilities. What have you always excelled at? In which classes have you felt confident and received good grades? It's your abilities in these areas that are making you distinctive—go with them. They're what will bring you rewards, financial and personal, in your work life as well.

Step 3: Investigate

Once you begin leaning in the direction of a possible field of study, investigate it by asking:

First, what can I do with a major in that area? Take electrical engineering, for example. Most people think of a generic situation in which an electrical engineer is solving problems having to do with electricity. Actually, a bachelor's degree in double-E can lead to these careers:

communications engineer, electrical engineer, power/solid state engineer, applications engineer, marketing engineer, construction and operator engineer, electrical test engineer, electronics engineer, electronics test engineer, systems engineer. And the outlook for all of these careers is good to excellent.

Second, how good is the college's program in that major? Any major you're considering at a particular institution should offer course work that runs the gamut from the introductory level to the highly sophisticated or challenging. There also should be opportunities to specialize in subtopics: not just English literature, for instance, but nineteenth-century women writers, too.

Step 4: Participate

Many colleges and universities offer special programs which are intended to help students gain practical experience in a career field or refine their ideas about their major field of study. Some of these special programs are:

Graduate courses open to undergraduates: Qualified undergraduates may take some graduate courses for credit.

Cooperative Education Program: Formal arrangements with off-campus employers allow students to combine work and study. A cooperative program may be designed as alternating (work and study in alternating terms) or parallel (work and study scheduled in the same term).

Intern Program: Students work in an occupation that interests them, usually during summer or mid-winter break. Sometimes the experience gained will be acceptable as college credit.

3-2 Degree Program: A program of liberal arts study for three years followed by two years of study in a professional field at another institution (or in a division of the same institution). Students graduate with two bachelor's degrees or a bachelor's and a master's.

Step 5: Concentrate

By the time you start firming up your major, concentrate! Resist the temptation to take courses that are only vaguely related to your major, or are of questionable application. When you graduate, you want your knowledge of a subject to be complete, accurate, and up to date. Steer away from courses that are known around campus as gut courses, puff courses, gases (instead of solids), or flaky courses. Stick to what will really benefit you in the long run.

A book that will help your child see the connections between a college major and his or her future work is *College to Career: The Guide to Job Opportunities,* by Joyce Slayton Mitchell (New York: College Entrance Examination Board, 1986).

A Word About Liberal Arts Degrees

Some parents worry that if their children major in liberal arts—music, philosophy, art history, English, for instance—they'll have trouble getting a job after college. Actually, a liberal arts education, as a general introduction to human culture, does a number of important things. It enhances a person's ability to express himself clearly, to analyze what other people say, to understand other people's behavior, and to make judgments based on reason. It's revealing that all the different kinds of graduate schools—among them law, medicine, and business—grant the largest percentage of their acceptances to students with majors in the humanities.

But why not listen to an appraisal of the value of a liberal arts education from an *employer,* whose bottom line is whether someone can do the job? Sam Bittner is an Omaha businessman who wrote the following remarks as part of an opinion piece that appeared in *The Chronicle of Higher Education.*

I have owned a scrap-metal business for 35 years. A year ago, I hired a new manager with unusual qualifications. He has an educational background of history and English; he holds a master's degree in foreign languages, and speaks French and German fluently.

He knew nothing about the scrap metal business. I gave him one week of instruction, told him to make mistakes and then use intelligence, imagination, and logic. He has turned this into one of the most efficiently run metal industries in the Middle West.

My company took a contract to extract beryllium from a mine in Arizona. I called in several consulting engineers and asked, "Can you furnish a chemical or electrolytic process that can be used at the mine site to refine directly from the ore?" Back came a report saying that I was asking for the impossible—a search of the computer tapes had indicated that no such process existed.

I paid the engineers for their report. Then I hired a student from Stanford University who was home for the summer. He was majoring in Latin American history with a minor in philosophy. I gave him an airplane ticket and a credit card and told him, "Go to Denver and research the Bureau of Mines archives and locate a chemical process for the recovery of beryllium." He left on Monday. I forgot to tell him that I was sending him for the impossible.

He came back on Friday. He handed me a pack of notes and booklets and said, "Here is the process. It was developed 33 years ago at a government research station at Rolla, Missouri. And here are other processes for the recovery of mica, strontium, columbium, and yttrium, which also exist as residual ores that contain beryllium." After one week of research, he was making sounds like a metallurgical expert.

He is now back in school, but I am keeping track of him. When other companies are interviewing the engineering and business administration mechanics, I'll be there looking for that history-and-philosophy major. . . .

In my business I want people who have tangible qualities. Anyone can meet them. They are marching across the pages of books—poetry, history, and novels."

In an extensive 20-year study done by AT&T of its employees, "humanities and social science majors were found to be stronger than engineering majors and similar to business majors in administrative skills and motivation for advancement." In the area of interpersonal skills, liberal arts graduates were the strongest of all. Placement personnel at the University of California at Berkeley have noted that recruitment of liberal arts majors by business has increased significantly in recent years.

The message is clear: if some area of liberal arts is what attracts your child, be reassured that people who can think clearly, communicate well, and exercise creativity will always be in demand.

Your Child and the Future

Although I've tried as much as possible in this book to help you and your child examine all the career possibilities open to her or him, I hope one thing that has also been clear is that personal growth and meeting new challenges are important aspects of career exploration. I hope that you will continue to encourage your child to take new classes, apply for new jobs, and think in terms of *creative change*. The time is gone when, as my grandfather did, a person could stay in the same job for most of his or her adult life. Now, jobs change, new kinds of jobs appear, and new kinds of workers, too. For your child to cope with these changes, it won't take, as Lewis Carroll wrote, "all the running you can do to stay in the same place," but instead, the confidence to proceed with a sure and steady tread toward the future with its promise of new opportunities and rewards. Your encouragement and support will be critical in helping your child greet change with optimism and excitement.

Appendix:
Where To Get
More Information
About Careers

Books, Articles, and Pamphlets

Agricultural, Forestry, and Fishing Occupations

"Farmers." *Career Brief.* Largo, FL: Careers, 1983.

"Horticulturalist." *Career Summary.* Largo, FL: Careers, 1983.

Skurzynski, Gloria. *Safeguarding the Land: Women at Work in Parks, Forests, and Range Lands.* New York: Harcourt Brace Jovanovich, Inc., 1981.

Wille, Christopher M. *Forestry Careers.* Lincolnwood, IL: VGM Career Horizons, 1985.

Your Career in Agriculture Agribusiness. Alexandria, VA: The Future Farmers of America. FFA, no date.

Administrative Support Occupations, Including Clerical

Ettinger, B. *Opportunities in Office Occupations.* Lincolnwood, IL: VGM Career Horizons, 1986.

Morrow, Jodie Berlin and Myrna Lebov. *Not Just a Secretary.* New York: Wiley, 1984.

Munday, Marianne. *Opportunities in Word Processing Careers.* Lincolnwood, IL: VGM Career Horizons, 1985.

181

Porat, Frieda and Mimi Will. *Dynamic Secretary: A Practical Guide to Achieving Success as an Executive Assistant.* Englewood Cliffs, NJ: Prentice-Hall, 1983.

Steinberg, Eve P. *How to Get a Clerical Job in Government Service.* New York: Arco, 1983.

Computer and Mathematical Occupations

Brechner, Irv. *Getting Into Computers.* New York: Ballantine, 1983.

Brockman, Dorothy. *Exploring Careers in Computer Software.* New York: Rosen, 1985.

Cardoza, Anne and Suzee Vlk. *Robotics Career Handbook.* New York: Arco, 1985.

Career Associates. *Career Choices for Students of Computer Science.* New York: Walker, 1985.

Career Associates. *Career Choices for Students of Mathematics.* New York: Walker, 1985.

Kling, Julie. *Opportunities in Computer Science.* Lincolnwood, IL: VGM Career Horizons, 1984.

Lee, Mary and Richard S. Lee. *Exploring Careers in Robotics.* New York: Rosen, 1986.

Marrs, Texe W. *High Technology Careers.* Homewood, IL: Dow-Jones Irwin, 1986.

Morgan, Richard. *Opportunities in Microelectronics Careers.* Lincolnwood, IL: VGM Career Horizons, 1985.

Muller, Peter. *The Fast Track to the Top Jobs in Computer Careers.* New York: Putnam Publishing Group, 1983.

Neirper, Norman. *Opportunities in Data Processing Careers.* Lincolnwood, IL: VGM Career Horizons, 1984.

Professional Opportunities in Mathematical Sciences. Washington, DC: Mathematical Association of America. No date.

Spencer, Jean. *Exploring Careers as a Computer Technician.* New York: Rosen, 1985.

Weinstein, Bob. *140 High-Tech Careers.* New York: Collier Books, 1985.

Weintraub, Joseph. *Exploring Careers in the Computer Field.* New York: Rosen, 1983.

Winkler, Connie. *The Computer Careers Handbook.* New York: Arco, 1983.

Construction Occupations

Construction. Washington, DC: Associated General Contractors of America.

Jones, Marilyn. *Exploring Careers as a Carpenter.* New York: Rosen, 1985.

Jones, Marilyn. *Exploring Careers in Plumbing.* Lincolnwood, IL: VGM Career Horizons, 1985.

Lobb, Charlotte. *Exploring Careers in Apprenticeship.* New York: Rosen, 1985.

Sumichrast, Michael. *Opportunities in Building Construction Trades.* Lincolnwood, IL: VGM Career Horizons, 1982.

Wood, Robert. *Opportunities in Electrical Trades.* Lincolnwood, IL: VGM Career Horizons, 1982.

Engineers, Surveyors, and Architects

"Aerospace Engineer." *Career Brief.* Largo, FL: Careers, 1983.

"Architects." *Occupational Outlook Handbook.* Washington, DC: U.S. Department of Labor, 1986–87.

"Engineers, General." *Career Brief.* Largo, FL: Careers, 1983.

'Engineering." *The World Book Encyclopedia.* 1985 ed.

General Electric Company. *What's It Like to be an Engineer?* Fairfield, CT: General Electric, 1983.

Hagerty, Joseph D. *Opportunities in Civil Engineering.* Lincolnwood, IL: VGM Career Horizons, 1981.

Heer, John and Joseph D. Hagerty. *Opportunities in Engineering Technology.* Lincolnwood, IL: VGM Career Horizons, 1986.

"Industrial Engineers." Moravia, NY: Chronicle Occupational Brief, 1984.

"Metallurgical Engineer." *Career Brief.* Largo, FL: Careers, 1983.

Reyes-Guerra, David R. Fischer, and Alan M. Fischer. *Engineering/High-Tech Student's Handbook.* Princeton, NJ: Peterson's Guides, 1988.

Executive, Administrative, and Managerial Occupations

"Accountants and Auditors." *Occupational Outlook Handbook.* U.S. Department of Labor, Washington, DC: 1986–87.

Baxter, Neale. *Opportunities in Government Service.* Lincolnwood, IL: VGM Career Horizons, 1979.

Berman, Elaine. *Your Career in Local, State & Federal Government.* New York: Arco, 1981.

Deen, Robert. *Opportunities in Business Communication.* Lincolnwood, IL: VGM Career Horizons, 1987.

Gordon, Susan. *Your Career in Hotel Management.* New York: Arco, 1983.

Henkin, Shepard. *Opportunities in Hotel and Motel Management.* Lincolnwood, IL: VGM Career Horizons, 1985.

Kirk, Richard. *Exploring Careers in Hospital and Health Services Administration.* New York: Rosen, 1983.

Miller, Daniel. *Starting a Small Restaurant.* Boston: Harvard Common Press, 1983.

Paradis, Adrian. *Opportunities in Banking.* Lincolnwood, IL: VGM Career Horizons, 1986.

Place, Irene and Sylvia Plummer. *Women in Management.* Lincolnwood, IL: VGM Career Horizons, 1985.

Rosenthal, Irving J. *Exploring Careers in Accounting.* New York: Rosen, 1986.

Stumpf, Stephen A. *Careers in Business.* New York: Simon and Schuster, Inc., 1984.

Traynor, William J. *Opportunities in Personnel Management.* Lincolnwood, IL: VGM Career Horizons, 1983.

Food and Beverage Preparation

"Careers in Foodservice." Pittsburgh, PA: National Institute for the Foodservice Industry. No date.

Caprione, Carol Ann. *Opportunities in Food Services.* Lincolnwood, IL: VGM Career Horizons, 1985.

"Cooks and Chefs." *Occupational Outlook Handbook.* Washington, DC: U.S. Department of Labor, 1984.

"Food and Beverage Preparation and Service Occupations." *Occupational Outlook Handbook.* Washington, DC: U.S. Department of Labor, 1986–87.

"Food Service Supervisor." *Career Brief.* Largo, FL: Careers, 1983.

Health Diagnosing and Treating Practitioners

Bacotti, J. *Opportunities in Opticianry.* New York: Rosen, 1983.

Feder, Judith. *Exploring Careers in Medicine.* New York: Rosen, 1986.

Graham, Lawrence. *Your Ticket to Medical or Dental School: Getting In and Staying In.* New York: Bantam Books, 1985.

Heitzman, William Ray. *Opportunities in Sports Medicine.* Lincolnwood, IL: VGM Career Horizons, 1986.

Helping Hands: Horizons Unlimited in Medicine. Chicago: American Medical Association, 1983.

Karlin, Leonard. *Your Career in Allied Dental Professions.* New York: Arco, 1982.

Keyes, Fenton. *Opportunities in Psychiatry.* Lincolnwood, IL: VGM Career Horizons, 1982.

Kitchell, Frank. *Opportunities in Optometry.* Lincolnwood, IL: VGM Career Horizons, 1985.

Rickert, Jessica A. *Exploring Careers in Dentistry.* New York: Rosen, 1983.

Rucker, T. Donald and Martin D. Keller. *Planning Your Medical Career.* Garrett Park, MD: Garrett Park Press, 1986.

Schafer, R.C. *Opportunities in Chiropractic Health Care.* New York: Rosen, 1985.

Shangold, Jules. *Opportunities in a Podiatry Career.* Lincolnwood, IL: VGM Career Horizons, 1984.

Virshup, Bernard. *Coping in Medical School.* New York: Norton, 1985.

Williams, Ellen. *Opportunities in Gerontology Careers.* Lincolnwood, IL: VGM Career Horizons, 1987.

Wischnitzer, Saul. *Futures in Health: A Complete Career Guidance Handbook for Prospective Allied Health Professionals.* New York: Barron's, 1985.

Marketing and Sales Occupations

Grant, Edgar. *Exploring Careers in the Travel Industry.* New York: Rosen, 1984.

Haas, Kenneth. *Opportunities in Sales and Marketing.* Lincolnwood, IL: VGM Career Horizons, 1982.

Laskin, David. *Getting Into Advertising: A Career Guide.* New York: Ballantine, 1986.

Reilly, George. *Guide to Cruise Ship Jobs.* Babylon, NY: Pilot Books, 1986.

Rosenthal, David W. *Careers in Marketing.* Englewood Cliffs, NJ: Prentice-Hall, 1984.

Schrayer, Robert. *Opportunities in Insurance Careers.* Lincolnwood, IL: VGM Career Horizons, 1986.

Weinstein, Bob. *Breaking Into Sales.* New York: Arco, 1984.

Mechanics and Repairers

Hammer, Hy. *Mechanical Ability Tests.* New York: Arco, 1984.

"Mechanics and Repair Technicians." *Career Summary.* Largo, FL: Careers, 1983.

"Mechanics and Repairers." *Occupational Outlook Handbook.* Washington, DC: U.S. Department of Labor, 1986–87.

Weber, Robert M. *Opportunities in Automotive Service.* Lincolnwood, IL: VGM Career Horizons, 1984.

Military Occupations

Bradley, Jeff. *Young Person's Guide to Military Service.* Boston: Harvard Common Press, 1983.

Betterton, Donald M. *How the Military Will Help You Pay for College.* Princeton, NJ: Peterson's Guides, 1985.

Cassidy, William. *How to Get Into US Service Academies.* New York: Arco, 1987.

Collins, Robert F. *The Reserve Officer Training Corps.* New York: Rosen, 1986.

Gordon, Susan. *Your Career in the Military.* New York: Arco, 1983.

Marrs, Texe and Karen Read. *Every Woman's Guide to Military Service.* Orom, UT: Liberty, 1984.

Perez, Dennis D. *The Enlisted Soldier's Guide.* Harrisburg, PA: Stackpole, 1986.

Slappey, Mary. *Exploring Military Service for Women.* New York: Rosen, 1986.

Nurses, Pharmacists, Dieticians, Therapists, and Physicians' Assistants

D'Orazio, Leo and Donald I. Snook, Jr. *Opportunities in Health and Medical Careers.* Lincolnwood, IL: VGM Career Horizons, 1983.

Downs, Florence. *New Careers in Nursing.* New York: Arco, 1983.

Frederickson, Keville. *Opportunities in Nursing.* Lincolnwood, IL: VGM Career Horizons, 1985.

Heron, Jackie. *Exploring Careers in Nursing.* New York: Rosen, 1986.

Kane, June K. *Exploring Careers in Dietetics & Nutrition.* New York: Rosen, 1987.

Krumhanl, Bernice R. *Opportunities in Physical Therapy.* Lincolnwood, IL: VGM Career Horizons, 1987.

Swanson, Barbara. *Careers in Health Care.* Homewood, IL: Dow-Jones Irwin, 1984.

200 Ways to Put Your Talent to Work in The Health Field. New York: National Health Council, 1987.

Part Time and Summer Jobs

Hawes, Gene R. *Going to College While Working.* New York: College Entrance Examination Board, 1985.

Lee, Patricia. *Complete Guide to Job Sharing.* New York: Walker, 1983.

Paradis, Adrian. *Opportunities in Part Time and Summer Jobs.* Lincolnwood, IL: VGM Career Horizons, 1987.

1987 Summer Employment Directory. Cincinnati: Writer's Digest. Published annually.

Physical Scientists and Life Scientists

A Career in Astronomy. New York: American Astronomical Society.

"Careers in Botany." Lexington, MA: Botanical Society of America.

Easton, Thomas. *Careers for Science.* Homewood, IL: Dow-Jones Irwin, 1984.

Heitzman, William Ray. *Opportunities in Marine & Maritime Careers.* Lincolnwood, IL: VGM Career Horizons, 1986.

Janovy, John, Jr. *On Becoming a Biologist.* New York: Harper & Row, 1985.

Lee, Mary P. and Richard Lee. *Opportunities in Animal and Pet Careers.* Lincolnwood, IL: VGM Career Horizons, 1984.

Martin, Gail M. "Science and Your Career." *Occupational Outlook Quarterly,* 26, 1983: 23–27.

Price, Mary Lee. *Exploring Careers in Research & Development.* New York: Rosen, 1983.

Ricciuti, Edward. *They Work With Wildlife.* New York: Harper & Row, 1983.

Rossbacher, Lisa A. *Career Opportunities in Geology and the Earth Sciences.* New York: Arco, 1983.

Shapiro, Stanley Jay. *Exploring Careers in Science.* New York: Rosen, 1986.

Winter, Charles A. *Opportunities in Biological Sciences.* Lincolnwood, IL: VGM Career Horizons, 1985.

Production Occupations

Bell, John A., and Lonny D. Garvey. *Opportunities in the Machine Trades.* Lincolnwood, IL: VGM Career Horizons, 1986.

Borowsky, Irving. *Opportunities in Printing Careers.* Lincolnwood, IL: VGM Career Horizons, 1985.

Lobb, Charlotte. *Exploring Careers in Apprenticeship.* New York: Rosen, 1985.

Protective Service Occupations

Baker, Mark. *Cops: Their Lives in Their Own Words.* New York: Simon and Schuster, 1985.

Coleman, Joseph. *Your Career in Law Enforcement.* New York: Arco, 1979.

Coleman, Ronny J. *Opportunities in Fire Protection Service.* Lincolnwood, IL: VGM Career Horizons, 1984.

Neal, Harry. *Secret Service in Action.* New York: Lodestar, 1980.

Steinberg, Eve P. *You as a Law Enforcement Officer.* New York: Arco, 1985.

Stinchcomb, James. *Opportunities in Law Enforcement and Criminal Justice.* Lincolnwood, IL: VGM Career Horizons, 1986.

Recreation and Leisure

Clary, Jack. *Careers in Sports.* Chicago, IL: Contemporary Books, 1982.

Figler, Stephen and Howard Figler. *The Athlete's Game Plan for College and Career.* Princeton, NJ: Peterson's Guides, 1985.

Heitzman, Ray. *Opportunities in Sports Medicine.* Lincolnwood, IL: VGM Career Horizons, 1986.

Jensen, Clayne R. and Jay H. Naylor. *Opportunities in Recreation and Leisure.* Lincolnwood, IL: VGM Career Horizons, 1984.

Odums, R. I. *Career Guide to Sports Officiating.* Cleveland, OH: Circular Limited, 1984.

Social Scientists, Social Workers, Religious Workers, and Lawyers

Berman, Elaine. *Your Career in Local, State and Federal Government.* New York: Arco, 1985.

Career Associates. *Career Choices for Students of Economics.* New York: Walker, 1985.

Career Associates. *Career Choices for Students of History.* New York: Walker, 1985.

Cornelius, Hal. *Career Guide for Paralegals.* New York: Monarch, 1983.

DeRidder, Margaret Djerf. *New Career Opportunities in Health and Human Services.* New York: Arco, 1984.

Fins, Alice. *Opportunities in Paralegal Careers.* Lincolnwood, IL: VGM Career Horizons, 1979.

Geography: Tomorrow's Career. Washington, DC: Association of American Geographers, 1983.

Glotzer, Arline. *Monarch's Complete Guide to Law School.* New York: Monarch, 1982.

Graham, Lawrence. *Your Ticket to Law School: Getting In and Staying In.* New York: Bantam, 1985.

Munnuke, Gary. *Opportunities in Law Careers.* Lincolnwood, IL: VGM Career Horizons, 1986.

Nadler, Burton. *Liberal Arts Jobs.* Princeton, NJ: Peterson's, 1986.

Nelson, John. *Opportunities in Religious Service.* Lincolnwood, IL: VGM Career Horizons, 1980.

"Religious Workers." *Occupational Outlook Handbook.* Washington, DC: U.S. Department of Labor, 1986–87.

Shanahan, William F. *101 Challenging Government Jobs for College Graduates.* New York: Arco, 1986.

Sigel, Louis S. *Exploring Careers in Public and Community Health.* New York: Rosen, 1984.

The Many Career Opportunities in Social Work. Silver Spring, MD: National Association of Social Workers, 1983.

What is Anthropology? Washington, DC: American Anthropological Association, 1982.

Teachers, Counselors, Librarians, Archivists, and Curators

Arnold, Edwin P. *Opportunities in Foreign Language Careers.* Lincolnwood, IL: VGM Career Horizons, 1986.

Baxter, Neale A. *Opportunities in Counseling and Development.* Lincolnwood, IL: VGM Career Horizons, 1986.

Career Associates. *Career Choices for Students of Psychology.* New York: Walker, 1985.

Edwards, E.W. *Careers in Using Foreign Language.* New York: Rosen, 1986.

Hahn, Lynn and James Hahn. *Exploring Careers in Home Economics.* New York: Rosen, 1981.

Heim, Kathleen and Peggy Sullivan. *Opportunities in Library and Information Science.* Lincolnwood, IL: VGM Career Horizons, 1985.

Ispa, Jean. *Exploring Careers in Child Care Service.* New York: Rosen, 1986.

Library and Information Careers in the 80's. Chicago: American Library Association, 1983.

Wittenberg, Renée. *Opportunities in Child Care Careers.* Lincolnwood, IL: VGM Career Horizons, 1987.

Writers, Artists, and Entertainers

Berlyn, David W. *Exploring Careers in Cable TV.* New York: Rosen, 1985.

Berryhill, Ken. *Funny Business: A Professional Guide to Becoming a Comic.* Englewood Cliffs, NJ: Prentice-Hall, 1985.

Bienstock, June. *Careers in Fact or Fiction.* Chicago: American Library Association, 1985.

Bone, Jan. *Opportunities in Telecommunications.* Lincolnwood, IL: VGM Career Horizons, 1984.

Brommer, Gerald F. *Careers in Art: An Illustrated Guide.* Worcester, MA: Davis, 1984.

Career Associates. *Career Choices for Students of Art.* New York: Walker, 1984.

Carr, Kale. *How You Can Star in TV Commercials.* New York: Rawson Wade, 1982.

Carter, Robert. *Opportunities in Book Publishing Careers.* Lincolnwood, IL: VGM Career Horizons, 1987.

Casewit, Curtis. *Freelance Writing: Advice from the Pros.* New York: Collier, 1985.

"Communication Occupations." *Occupational Outlook Handbook.* Washington, DC: U.S. Department of Labor, 1986–87.

Deckinger, E. L. *Exploring Careers in Advertising.* New York: Rosen, 1986.

Dolber, Roslyn. *Opportunities in Fashion Careers.* Lincolnwood, IL: VGM Career Horizons, 1986.

Field, Shelly. *Career Opportunities in the Music Industry.* New York: Facts on File, 1986.

Gearhart, Susan W. *Opportunities in Modeling Careers.* Lincolnwood, IL: VGM Career Horizons, 1984.

Greenberg, Jon W. *Theater Careers: A Comprehensive Guide to Non-Acting Careers in the Theater.* New York: Holt, Rinehart and Winston, 1983.

Henry, Mari Lyn and Lynne Reyers. *How to be a Working Actor: The Insider's Guide to Finding Jobs in Theater, Film, and Television.* New York: Evans, 1986.

Jabenis, Elaine. *Fashion Directors.* New York: John Wiley, 1983.

Lulow, Joann. *Your Career in the Fashion Industry.* New York: Arco, 1979.

Munschauer, John L. *Jobs for English Majors and Other Smart People.* Princeton, NJ: Peterson's Guides, 1986.

Noronha, Shonan. *Careers in Communications.* Lincolnwood, IL: VGM Career Horizons, 1987.

Reed, Maxine K. and Robert M. Reed. *Career Opportunities in Television, Cable and Video.* New York: Facts on File, 1986.

Vahl, Rod. *Careers in Broadcast Journalism.* New York: Rosen, 1983.

Weinstein, Bob. *Breaking into Communication.* New York: Arco, 1984.

Zacharis, John C. *Exploring Careers in Communications & Television.* New York: Rosen, 1985.

Zeller, Susan L. *Your Career in Radio & Television Broadcasting.* New York: Arco, 1982.

Special Interest Magazines

Animals

Animal Kingdom, New York Zoological Park, Bronx, NY 10460. Bimonthly magazine for members of zoological societies, individuals interested in wildlife, zoos, and aquariums.

Bird Talk, Fancy Publications, Box 6050, Mission Viejo, CA 92690. Monthly magazine covering the care and training of cage birds for men and women who own any number of pet or exotic birds.

Cats Magazine, Box 10766, Southport, NC 28461. Monthly magazine for men and women of all ages; cat enthusiasts, vets, and geneticists.

Dog Fancy, Fancy Publications, Inc., Box 6050, Mission Viejo, CA 92690. Monthly magazine for men and women of all ages interested in all phases of dog ownership.

Horse & Rider Magazine, Rich Publishing, Inc., 41919 Moreno Road, Temecula, CA 92390. Monthly magazine for horse owners, riders, breeders, and trainers.

Tropical Fish Hobbyist, TFH Publications, Inc., 211 West Sylvania Avenue, Neptune City, NJ 07753. Monthly magazine covering the tropical fish hobby.

Automotive and Motorcycle

Car Craft, Petersen Publishing Company, 8490 Sunset Boulevard, Los Angeles, CA 90069. Magazine for young men and women interested in racing, automobile shows, and car maintenance.

Cycle, Ziff-Davis Publishing Company, 780-A Lakefield Road, Westlake Village, CA 91361. Monthly magazine for motorcycle owners and enthusiasts.

Cycle World, 1499 Monrovia Avenue, Newport Beach, CA 92663. Monthly magazine for motorcycle owners and enthusiasts.

Hot Rod, Petersen Publishing Company, 8490 Sunset Boulevard, Los Angeles, CA 90069. For readers primarily interested in racing and high performance street machines.

Road & Track, 1499 Monrovia Avenue, Newport Beach, CA 92663. For car enthusiasts.

Art

Arts Magazine, 23 East 26th Street, New York, NY 10010. Journal of contemporary art, art criticism, analysis, and history, particularly for artists, scholars, museum officials, art teachers and students, and collectors.

Fiberarts, The Magazine of Textiles, 50 College Street, Asheville, NC 28801. Bimonthly magazine covering textiles as art and craft for textile artists, craftspeople, hobbyists, teachers, museum and gallery staffs, collectors and enthusiasts.

Glass Craft News, The Monthly Magazine for Stained Glass Enthusiasts, Edge Publishing Group, Room 1310, 270 Lafayette Street, New York, NY 10012. Bimonthly magazine covering stained glass.

Metalsmith, Society of North American Goldsmiths, 6707 North Santa Monica Boulevard, Milwaukee, WI 53217-3940. Quarterly magazine covering craft metalwork and metal arts for people who work in metal and those interested in the field.

Aviation

Private Pilot, Fancy Publications, Inc., Box 6050, Mission Viejo, CA 92690. For owners and/or pilots of private aircraft, for student pilots and others aspiring to attain additional ratings and experience.

General Aviation News, Box 110918, Carrollton, TX 75006. For pilots, aviation buffs, aircraft owners, aircraft dealers, and related business people.

College and Career

The Black Collegian, Black Collegiate Services, Inc., 1240 South Broad Street, New Orleans, LA 70125. Magazine for black college students and recent graduates with an interest in black cultural awareness, sports, news, personalities, history, trends, current events, and job opportunities.

Collegiate Career Woman, Equal Opportunity Publications, Inc., 44 Broadway, Greenlawn, NY 11740. Magazine covering career guidance for college women.

Health and Fitness

American Health Magazine, American Health Partners, 80 Fifth Avenue, New York, NY 10011. General interest magazine that covers both scientific and lifestyle aspects of health.

Shape, Weider Enterprises, 21100 Erwin Street, Woodland Hills, CA 91367. Monthly magazine covering women's health and fitness.

Hobby and Craft

The Antique Trader Weekly, Box 1050, Dubuque, IA 52001. Weekly newspaper for collectors and dealers in antiques and collectibles.

Coins, Krause Publications, 700 East State Street, Iola, WI 54990. Monthly magazine about U.S. and foreign coins for all levels of collectors, investors, and dealers.

Gems and Minerals, Box 687, Mentone, CA 92359. Monthly magazine for the professional and amateur gem cutter, jewelry maker, mineral collector, and rockhound.

Live Steam, Live Steam, Inc. 2779 Aero Park Drive, Box 629, Traverse City, MI 49685. Monthly magazine covering steam-powered models and full-size engines.

Model Railroading, 1027 North 7th Street, Milwaukee, WI 53233. Monthly magazine for hobbyists interested in scale model railroading.

Numismatic News, Krause Publications, 700 East State Street, Iola, WI 54990. Tabloid newspaper on collecting U.S. coins.

Sports Collectors Digest, Krause Publications, 700 East State Street, Iola, WI 54990. Sports memorabilia magazine published 26 times a year.

The Woodworker's Journal, Madrigal Publishing Company, Inc., 517 Lichtfield Road, Box 1629, New Milford, CT 06776. Bimonthly magazine covering woodworking for woodworking hobbyists of all levels of skill.

Military

Army Magazine, 2425 Wilson Boulevard, Arlington, VA 22201. Monthly magazine emphasizing military interests.

Military Review, U.S. Army Command and General Staff College, Fort Leavenworth, KS 66027-6910. Monthly journal emphasizing the military for senior officers, students, and scholars.

Sea Power, 2300 Wilson Boulevard, Arlington, VA 22201. Monthly magazine for naval personnel and civilians interested in naval, maritime, and defense matters.

Music

Guitar Player Magazine, GPI Publications, 20085 Stevens Creek, Cupertino, CA 95014. Monthly magazine about guitar performance, equipment, and music careers.

Modern Drummer, 870 Pompton Avenue, Cedar Grove, NJ 07009. For drummers of all ages and abilities.

Modern Recording & Music, MR&M Publishing Corporation, 1120 Old Country Road, Plainview, NY 11803. Monthly magazine covering semi-pro and professional recording of music for musicians, soundmen, and recording engineers.

Nature, Conservation, and Ecology

Audubon Magazine, 950 Third Avenue, New York, NY 10022. Monthly magazine for nature enthusiasts.

International Wildlife, National Wildlife Federation, 1412 16th Street NW, Washington, DC 20036. Bimonthly magazine for persons interested in natural history.

Natural History, Natural History Magazine, 79th and Central Park West, New York, NY 10024. Monthly magazine for ecologically aware audience.

Sierra, The Sierra Club Bulletin, 530 Bush Street, San Francisco, CA 94108. Published six times a year for people interested in conservation and environmental politics.

Personal Computing

Byte Magazine, 70 Main Street, Peterborough, NH 03458. Monthly magazine covering personal computers.

Infoworld, Popular Computing, Inc., Suite 305, 530 Lytton Avenue, Palo Alto, CA 94301. Weekly magazine covering personal computers, personal computing, and the computer industry.

MacWorld, PC World Communications, Inc., 555 DeHaro Street, San Francisco, CA 94107. Magazine covering use of Apple's MacIntosh computer.

PC World, PC World Communications, Inc., 555 DeHaro Street, San Francisco, CA 94107. Monthly magazine covering IBM personal computers and compatibles.

Photography

Petersen's Photographic Magazine, Petersen Publishing Co., 8490 Sunset Boulevard, Los Angeles, CA 90069. Monthly magazine emphasizing how-to photography.

Popular Photography, 1 Park Avenue, New York, NY 10016. Monthly magazine for advanced and professional photographers.

Science

CQ: The Radio Amateur's Journal, 76 North Broadway, Hicksville, NY 11801. Monthly journal for amateur radio community.

Modern Electronics, Modern Electronics Publishing, Inc., 76 North Broadway, Hicksville, NY 11801. Monthly magazine for readers interested in personal computers, circuitry, and electronic technology.

Popular Science, 380 Madison Avenue, New York, NY 10017. Monthly magazine for readers interested in science and new products.

Science Digest, Hearst Magazines Division, Hearst Corporation, 888 7th Avenue, New York, NY 10106. Monthly magazine emphasizing science and technology for all ages.

Theater, Movies, TV, and Entertainment

Dance Magazine, 33 West 60th Street, New York, NY 10023. Monthly magazine covering all aspects of dance.

Film Comment, Film Society of Lincoln Center, 140 West 65th Street, New York, NY 10023. Bimonthly magazine covering cinema.

Prevue, Prevue Entertainment, Box 974, Reading, PA 19603. Bimonthly magazine covering entertainment, films, TV, music, and books.

Theater Crafts Magazine, Theater Crafts Associates, 135 5th Avenue, New York, NY 10010. Monthly magazine about performing arts, video, and film, with the emphasis on production and design.

Index

Other Books of Interest from the College Board

003144 *Index of Majors, 1988–89.* Lists 500 majors at the 3,000 colleges and graduate institutions, state by state, that offer them. ISBN: 0-87447-314-4, $13.95 (Updated annually)

002911 *Profiles in Achievement,* by Charles M. Holloway. Traces the careers of eight outstanding men and women who used education as the key to later success. (Hardcover, ISBN: 0-87447-291-1, $15.95); 002857 paperback (ISBN: 0-87447-285-7, $9.95).

002598 *Succeed with Math,* by Sheila Tobias. A *practical* guide that helps students overcome math anxiety and gives them the tools for mastering the subject in high school and college courses as well as the world of work. ISBN: 0-87447-259-8, $12.95

003039 *10 SATs: Third Edition.* Ten actual, recently administered SATs plus the full text of *Taking the SAT,* the College Board's official advice. ISBN: 0-87447-303-9, $9.95

002571 *Writing Your College Application Essay,* by Sarah Myers McGinty. An informative and reassuring book that helps students write distinctive application essays and explains what colleges are looking for in these essays. ISBN: 0-87447-257-1, $9.95

002474 *Your College Application,* by Scott Gelband, Catherine Kubale, and Eric Schorr. A step-by-step guide to help students do their best on college applications. ISBN: 0-87447-247-4, $9.95

To order by direct mail any books not available in your local bookstore, please specify the item number and send your request with a check made payable to the College Board for the full amount to: College Board Publications, Department M53, Box 886, New York, New York 10101-0886. Allow 30 days for delivery. An institutional purchase order is required in order to be billed, and postage will be charged on all billed orders. Telephone orders are not accepted, but information regarding any of the above titles is available by calling Publications Customer Service at (212) 713-8165.